NO18 34			
MY 12 '95			
MY 11 '96			
MY 20 00			

DEMCO 38-296

Foreign Policy
in the
Reagan
Presidency

Foreign Policy
in the
Reagan
Presidency

Nine Intimate Perspectives

Sterling Kernek   Paul H. Nitze

Caspar Weinberger   John C. Whitehead

Max M. Kampelman   Elliott Abrams

Dwight Ink   Paul H. Nitze

Don Oberdorfer

Edited by

Kenneth W. Thompson

Volume III
The Miller Center Reagan Oral History Series

UNIVERSITY
PRESS OF
AMERICA

AUG   '94

The Miller Center

University of Virginia

Lanham • New York • London

Copyright © 1993 by
University Press of America®, Inc.
4720 Boston Way
Lanham, Maryland 20706

3 Henrietta Street
London WC2E 8LU England

Co-published by arrangement with
The Miller Center of Public Affairs,
University of Virginia

The views expressed by the author(s) of this publication do not necessarily
represent the opinions of the Miller Center. We hold to Jefferson's dictum that:
"Truth is the proper and sufficient antagonist to error, and has nothing to
fear from the conflict, unless by human interposition, disarmed of her
natural weapons, free argument and debate."

Library of Congress Cataloging-in-Publication Data

Foreign policy in the Reagan presidency : nine intimate perspectives /
Sterling Kernek . . . [et al.] ; edited by Kenneth W. Thompson.
p.   cm.
1. United States—Foreign relations—1981–1989. 2. Reagan,
Ronald. I. Kernek, Sterling J. II. Thompson, Kenneth W.
E876.F665   1993   327.73—dc20   93–7244 CIP

ISBN 0–8191–9087–X (cloth : alk. paper)
ISBN 0–8191–9088–8 (pbk. : alk. paper)

The paper used in this publication meets the minimum requirements of
American National Standard for Information Sciences—Permanence
of Paper for Printed Library Materials, ANSI Z39.48–1984.

To

the memory of

the Founders

of the Chicago School

who fashioned a Golden Age

for the study of American Foreign Policy

Hans J. Morgenthau

and

Quincy Wright

CONTENTS

PREFACE

One sign of the contemporaneity of the Reagan administration is the projected publication of four or five volumes on the Reagan presidency by the Miller Center. In approaching the Reagan oral history, we have reaped the benefits of participation by a larger number of witnesses and subjects than with any previous postwar presidency. With the Miller Center's Roosevelt oral history, no more than a half dozen high-ranking officials from that administration were available. With the greater availability of the Reagan official family, we have already exceeded 50 participants.

On the other side of this advantage, we lack the authoritative historical sources, the monographs and scholarly articles, and the reconsiderations or revisions that enrich the study of earlier presidencies. No point is served in discounting the benefits of historical perspective. Such perspective is clearly lacking in the search for truth in the 1980s. With the Reagan presidency, if not all postwar presidencies, we approach a historical era the end of which is not yet in sight. We are dealing with a story viewed only from its beginning, its midpoint, and a few high points. At best we have only the most fragmentary knowledge of the consequences. Our task is more complex because of the ideological divisions surrounding the Reagan presidency. Within and outside the administration, historians and scholars as well as policymakers cluster together around different value systems.

However, the limitation of sources and possible observer bias are nothing new in the annals of political history. James Madison wrote of such limits, saying:

It has been a misfortune of history that a *personal knowledge* and an *impartial judgment* of things can *rarely meet* in the historian. The best history of our country

ix

therefore must be the fruit of contributions bequeathed by contemporary actors and witnesses, to successors who will make an unbiased use of them.

But Madison took heart from the fact that future historians and scholars might find in such early histories the sources on which more detached and objective studies could be written. His optimism about historical interpretation is one we share. It lies at the center of our commitment to oral histories. We make bold to suggest that future historians of the Reagan administration will draw on these early findings. The participants in our inquiry have helped lay the foundations for future research.

Madison concluded:

And if the abundance and authenticity of the materials . . . should descend to hands capable of doing justice to them, then American history can be expected to contain more truth, and *lessons . . . not less valuable*, than that of *any country or age* whatever [italics added].

INTRODUCTION

The majority of the early studies of the Reagan administration cluster together under three main headings. Rather surprisingly, given their declarations of scientific objectivity, scholars with Reagan sympathies have organized early symposia and volumes of essays on the Reagan administration. Seeing their turf being challenged, journalists and pundits have contributed their own independent interpretations of an administration characterized from its beginnings by outspoken defenders and hostile critics. Finally, a few longtime observers of the political career of Ronald Reagan provide a third source of understanding. Perhaps the most respected is Lou Cannon of the *Washington Post*.

The present volume undertakes to build bridges between differing viewpoints. It seeks to marry the perceptions of historians such as Sterling Kernek with journalists like Don Oberdorfer, with diplomatists such as Paul H. Nitze, and with policymakers such as Caspar Weinberger and ambassador and counsel Max M. Kampelman. The present volume is the product of serious scholarship and firsthand observation by a group of well-respected leaders.

The hallmark of the Miller Center is its continuing emphasis on the union of theory and practice. Its Reagan volumes are examples of such research and study. The organization of *Foreign Policy in the Reagan Presidency* is a product of the Center's underlying point of view and approach.

Professor Sterling Kernek of Southern Illinois University is uniquely qualified to write on the Reagan foreign policy. He points to the wide-ranging conclusions of American scholars on the issue of whether Reagan's foreign policy was a success or failure. The great merit of his essay is its objective assessment of the different phases of Reagan's policy. In discussing the first phase, Kernek pays tribute to Reagan's ties with past administrations and their foreign policies. He demonstrates how Reagan's hard-line view of U.S.-Soviet relations continued from 1980 to 1983. However, Kernek cites evidence to show that the President from the beginning linked arms control negotiations with the buildup of U.S. strength, a formula reminiscent of former Secretary of State Dean Acheson's concept of "situations of strength." In his speeches, Reagan held out the possibility of genuine *arms limitation* contrasted with *arms control* in previous administrations. His predecessors set ceilings rather than reducing the total arms buildup. The change came in 1984, especially in his speech of 16 January 1984, when Reagan defined the three guiding principles of his arms limitation policy: realism, strength, and dialogue.

Into this policy context, the President introduced his dream of a strategic defense initiative. Widely criticized by prominent physicists and scientists as an unrealizable goal, Reagan used SDI in his negotiations with the Soviets while all the time denying it was or could ever become a bargaining chip in negotiations. At this point, Kernek introduces his own personal theory that Reagan had an uncanny ability to position himself so as to gain political advantages whatever the results of a given initiative. Linked with his unchanging optimism, this innate political skill enabled him to turn strategic disasters into political success.

Columnists who have followed the broad sweep of American foreign policy consider Paul H. Nitze one of the nation's most seasoned diplomatists. His public service began with the presidency of Franklin D. Roosevelt. His discussion provides much insight on President Reagan and the divisions within the Reagan administration. Of all the informative testimony in the Reagan oral history, Nitze's commentary on a host of personalities and issues is perhaps the most revealing. His vignettes of the early and later Reagan are especially instructive. From being relatively uninformed on national security policy, Reagan became an unrivaled spokesman for democracy against totalitarianism. He left the details to others in the implementation of his vision.

Mr. Nitze's candid evaluation of the programs and personalities of leading Reaganites involved in foreign policy and his assessment of the varied elements that make up the defense budget provide a textbook example of national security thinking. When challenged on the scope of the national defense, he explains that "we need a balanced capability to do things that are often unforeseeable." His evaluation of the strengths and limitations of the battleship, the B-1 and B-2 aircraft, and the Soviet radar system gives content to his overall analysis. He discusses how changes in the world have influenced our foreign policy choices and holds forth on both well-known and little-known forms of Soviet deception. In all his discussion of the Reagan foreign policy and the issues it confronted, Nitze combines tough-minded evaluation with obvious commitment to the administration.

Caspar Weinberger served with Governor Reagan in Sacramento and was secretary of defense in the Reagan administration. He speaks of President Reagan as one of the most underestimated political leaders in the world and suggests that this may have helped him negotiate with those with whom he had differences. Weinberger characterizes the President as "a man who enjoys life . . . likes people . . . and wants them to be comfortable and happy." He wrote many of his own speeches, including his best, Weinberger asserts. Reagan's experience as governor of California prepared him for the presidency. Weinberger praises Reagan's ability to pick men he trusted and depend on them to handle the details. His leadership style fit the presidency. "He was much more concerned with broad policy."

In discussing arms accords, Weinberger emphasizes the importance of results. He minimizes his differences with Secretary of State George Shultz. "Such differences exist in every administration." He makes mention of his criteria for the military involvement of American forces abroad, a subject that was the centerpiece of his speech to the National Press Club. They included never entering a war that we didn't intend to win and never entering unless we felt it was important enough that we had to win, unless we intended to support the troops, and unless we were willing to do everything possible in order to win. He was pleased with the Bush strategy in the Gulf War and in Panama, which corresponded with his own personal philosophy. He spells out his criteria for compromise in arms agreements and compares that with the attitude of the State Department.

Part II is devoted to issues of Reagan's personality and policy-making. John C. Whitehead had a long and impressive career as an investment banker at Goldman, Sachs & Company before joining the Reagan administration. He recounts the story of his appointment as deputy secretary of state because it gives such a vivid picture of President Reagan. It is a story that helps to portray Reagan's decisiveness and toughness in important negotiations. He succeeded not only in persuading Whitehead to accept but convinced him he should cancel an important visit and speaking engagement in Tokyo in order to meet the President's exacting timetable. Whitehead observes that "you could sense his inner strength that was not always visible."

Another incident reported by Secretary Whitehead concerns his meeting with President Bettino Craxi of Italy on the eve of a meeting of the "Big Seven" in Washington. The Italian leader and President Reagan were sensitive about their different views on the handling of the *Achille Lauro* incident and the Italian release of the terrorist leader Abu Abbas. Whitehead flew to Rome, met with President Craxi, and, sensing that personal and national ego were involved, allowed Craxi to read proudly from a text for an hour and 15 minutes on the role he had played and the rationale behind the Italian strategy. In Whitehead's words, that "let the air out of the balloon" and Craxi agreed to leave almost immediately for the "Big Seven" meeting.

Another event was the reaction of top U.S. officials to the so-called "surgical strike" against Gadhafi's Libya. At a meeting chaired by President Reagan, the secretary of defense, the chairman of the Joint Chiefs, the deputy secretary of state, and eight congressional leaders all expressed their views. Some expressed reservations, but the President himself made the controversial decision to go forward with the strike. Whitehead also provides his own version of one aspect of the Iran-contra dispute and the President's gentle reprimand of his deputy secretary for having given an honest but imprudent answer to a question in televised hearings on the dispute.

Secretary Whitehead's wonderful candor breaks through again in his description of a meeting with Saddam Hussein in Iraq, who he felt at the time was superior to other Arab leaders. In conclusion, Whitehead responds to a series of questions, most of which throw light on Reagan's character and policy-making. On another issue, Whitehead speaks of a world environmental conference whose task was the reduction of hydrocarbons. Whitehead went to the President and pointed out that the United States had an opportunity to control the pollutants that were causing a hole in the ozone layer. The State Department had come under attack from the far right and the deputy secretary asked if they spoke for the President. President Reagan responded that he was not against a treaty. All these examples suggest the possibility of a revisionist view of the Reagan presidency that may or may not follow these preliminary estimates.

The second chapter in Part II on "Personality and Policy-making" begins with a question addressed to Ambassador Max Kampelman. One of America's most respected lawyers, Kampelman proved to be a skillful negotiator on arms limitation treaties. He came to know a variety of Soviet negotiators; he was able to measure their attitudes and their style. Ambassador Kampelman had an introduction to Communists as negotiators within the Democratic Farmer Labor party in Minnesota. In the text of his paper, Kampelman is asked about institutional relations for arms control. What were his relationships with the secretary of state and the President? What were his impressions of the President when they first met and toward the end of their relations? The Kampelman essay is rich in insights on personalities and policies. The value of Kampelman's response is his combining of general principles with specific historical examples. The continuity of Kampelman's experiences from Minnesota to negotiating with the Soviets on arms control is a chronicle in American politics and law that enhances understanding of the Reagan foreign policy.

At the outset of his contribution, Assistant Secretary Elliott Abrams quotes a State Department official who characterized President Reagan's leadership style as that of "a mysterious man." In the same vein, Abrams suggests that Reagan was "a terrific president but not a terrific prime minister." By that he means that Reagan was an inspirational and symbolic leader of the people but not an effective manager of the government's institutions. Despite

Reagan's prior experience as governor of California, he was not a good administrator.

Abrams reviews a series of episodes in which the President participated involving Panama and Central America. In some, he showed awareness of all sides of the argument and had few doubts about his own point of view. In others, he laid back and did little to resolve important controversies, say, between State and Defense. Sometimes he temporized and withdrew. Other times he may have favored one group or viewpoint but couldn't bring himself to oppose the other. In certain cases, he allowed one side to win by default. Abrams also discusses the President's memory, which was strongest on issues that mattered most to him and quite limited on issues about which he had no strong feeling. Finally, Abrams discusses at length a whole set of issues raised in Iran-contra and the future of Nicaragua as well as on human rights, the use of force, the Soviet collapse, and relations between Shultz and Weinberger.

Abrams returns to the point that Reagan was not a good administrator and asks why the Reagan administration, with a few exceptions, worked relatively well. One of the reasons was that the President gave ideological or political guidance, and this conditioned the struggles that went on at lower levels of the administration. Reagan's guidance allowed for the appointment of Scoop Jackson-type Democrats whom Reagan considered fell within his ideological guidelines. Subordinates also knew what the issues were on which they could press their policy viewpoint, for example, Central America. They also recognized other issues on which the President did not share an assistant's enthusiasm, as with human rights in Chile. Finally, Abrams concludes by defending his own confrontational approach in defending Central American and human rights policies.

As the lead author in Part III, Dwight Ink, one of the nation's respected senior authorities on public administration, was a member of the Policy Committee of the President-elect's transition team with responsibility for recommending the organization and management of the incoming administration. He also advised on such issues as the organization of the Cabinet and whether or not there should be permanent Departments of Education and Energy. He recounts the story of the dismantling of one agency—the

Community Service Administration—and his recommendations on how and by whom this should be accomplished. He also tells of his experiences as head of the General Services Administration (GSA). Following that, Dr. Ink's next assignment was as an assistant administrator for the Agency for International Development (AID) responsible for the Western Hemisphere assistance program.

Until his AID experience, Ink's comments on relations with the Reagan White House were positive, but AID provided negative lessons. He explained that this resulted from White House timidity and belligerency toward Congress. Not only congressional relations, but the substance of Ink's work—narcotics—and the way it was handled caused him concern. He writes of the justice system in Colombia, its limited communications system, and kidnappings and torture by the terrorists. His complaint against the Reagan National Security Council was that it was the least effective one he had seen during his long career in Washington. He attempts to show how the NSC underestimated the importance of economic assistance. The most revealing account of the Reagan administration's approach to technical assistance is Ink's experience in holding up economic support funds. In response to questions, Dr. Ink responds in ways that provide an overall picture of Reagan.

Paul H. Nitze contributes a second essay in which he acknowledges changes in his perception of Mr. Reagan. Nitze goes on to assess Reagan's behavior at the Reykjavík conference. Nitze discusses his opposition to arms reductions by equal percentages and his preference for an equal outcome in the weapons of the two sides. When Nitze discovered opposition to his approach among his six advisers, he raised the issue in the middle of the night with Secretary of State Shultz. The secretary told Nitze to run the negotiations the way he wished, and Nitze and a representative of the White House who had accompanied him returned to the table. Negotiations went on until Foreign Minister Shevardnadze inserted SDI back into the discussion. Nitze makes the interesting point that what he and others had meant was the total elimination of ballistic missiles, whereas President Reagan confused it with the total elimination of strategic nuclear weapons. Nitze offers a more positive evaluation of Reykjavík than others who discuss it in the oral history.

INTRODUCTION

Don Oberdorfer is the author of *The Turn: From the Cold War to a New Era.* He discusses the ending of the Cold War and the little-known story of the role of particular Soviet and American leaders. He views his essay as a contribution in contemporary history or what he calls "the second draft of history," journalism being the first. He tries to measure Reagan's input and Shultz's, as well as Gorbachev's and Shevardnadze's role. The account reads like a fascinating novel but a factual one. I leave it to the reader to discover for himself or herself Oberdorfer's explanation of the ending of the Cold War, which is the concluding essay in the volume.

I

PRINCIPLES
OF FOREIGN POLICY

CHAPTER 1

REAGAN'S FOREIGN POLICY LEADERSHIP*

STERLING KERNEK

NARRATOR: Professor Kernek was a visiting scholar at the Miller Center from 1987-88. He received his bachelor's degree at American University and his master's degree from the University of Western Australia. He studied in England with Professor F. H. Hinsley and earned a Ph.D. from Cambridge University in England. At Western Illinois University, where he is a Professor of History, he has proven himself the kind of faculty member that every university department hopes for, but few discover. He has been director of the honors program, a member of the committee that reformed the general education curriculum, and has carried out many other assignments with dedication and skill.

Kernek has written widely on World War I, notably a book entitled *Distractions of Peace During War: The Lloyd George Government's Reaction to Woodrow Wilson, December 1916 - November 1918.* He's authored articles on a range of subjects: Frederick Jackson Turner's frontier theory of history, Henry Kissinger, the comparative history of Australia and America, and Wilson's idea of national self-determination. He's the author of an article in the *Virginia Quarterly Review* entitled "Historical Reflections on the Dangers Ahead" and in 1985 co-authored another scholarly paper in the *Political Science Quarterly* entitled, "How Realistic is Reagan's Diplomacy?"

---

*Presented in a Forum at the Miller Center on 16 August 1989.

The debate about the Reagan presidency has already begun. A very interesting aspect of it is the argument of Fred Greenstein, who while at the Miller Center completed the first major revisionist work on Eisenhower entitled *The Hidden-Hand Presidency*. Greenstein maintains that Reagan never delegated effectively and didn't demonstrate the skills that Greenstein found in Eisenhower. Subsequently, Greenstein wrote an article that advanced the same thesis. On the other hand, Lou Cannon, writing in the *Washington Post*, has begun to ask whether we will find, when we look carefully at the Reagan presidency, that President Reagan, like President Eisenhower, was much more on top of the details of policy than was assumed.

From the first years of the Reagan presidency Professor Kernek has been writing about the Reagan foreign policy. Since he is also an alumnus of the Center, it is proper that he initiate our discussion of Reagan's foreign policy.

MR. KERNEK: You are correct that people are already lining up in the assessment of the Reagan presidency. I was looking at some writings yesterday and the contrast is amazing. Here, on one hand, is a piece that was in the *Virginia Quarterly Review*. You get a sense of the article by the title, "Decisions in the Land of Pretend: U.S. Foreign Policy in the Reagan Years" by James Nathan. It describes Reagan's policy in terms of comedy and chaos and being asleep at the switch. It quotes Haig's idea of the administration as a ghost ship where you catch glimpses of the crew, but you don't know who is really guiding the ship. On the other hand, here is a very interesting piece by a professor at Berkeley, Aaron Wildavsky, who says nothing less than, "Reagan remains the most creative President in recent times, and with Franklin Roosevelt, one of the two most influential of the modern era." It's hard to imagine a greater contrast of views between serious scholars.

Supporters and admirers of President Reagan have emphasized the results of his Soviet policy, and they can point to mounting evidence that his policy was successful. The trend of events clearly seemed to be going his way at the end of his presidency. Many observers, of course, point out the contrast between Reagan's first term and his second term. He seemed to take a very hard line in the first term. He switched his tone in 1984, and then we entered what he himself described as a new era.

It was remarkable to see him at the Moscow summit in 1988. When he was asked about his highly publicized references to the "evil empire," he simply replied that this was another time and another era. He went on to claim during the rest of that year that in fact his basic principles had been vindicated. Thus, we have this issue of real change in Reagan but also a claim to consistency. My own position is as follows: I consider Reagan a kind of a hard-line romantic, but I also have admiration for his qualities as a politician and statesman.

During the period from 1981 through the end of 1983, Reagan was following basically a hard-line stance in relations with the Soviet Union. Nonetheless, he made some significant modifications. Presidents often come into power claiming that they are establishing new policies. Historians and political scientists looking back on these claims often note that there are a lot of continuities between presidencies. Robert Osgood put it rather well when he said that "The continuities of American foreign policy are always greater than the political claims to innovation would have one believe." To be sure changes occur, but much of it has a familiar rhythm. Osgood described the oscillation in America's world role between assertion and retrenchment. In the postwar years, this change was between an assertive American foreign policy and a foreign policy of retrenchment. It has tended to reflect perceived changes in the Soviet threat.

When Reagan came into power, there was a fairly broad consensus on the Soviet threat in the country. Reagan responded by championing a massive military buildup, and he accompanied the buildup with rhetoric reminiscent of the old Cold War years. Books began to appear talking about a new Cold War or of a revival of the Cold War. During his election campaign, Reagan had projected the vision that America would stand tall and turn back the rising Soviet threat. He reaffirmed the doctrine of linkage in dealing with Moscow, indicating that any progress on arms control should coincide with moderation of Soviet imperialism in the Third World.

In an early interview with Walter Cronkite in March 1981 he cited Soviet aggression in Afghanistan, subversion in Central America, and intervention by Soviet surrogates—the Cubans in Angola, the East Germans in Ethiopia and so on. He explained that he was going to re-arm the United States, and one of the purposes was to strengthen its bargaining positions in arms control.

He was still interested in arms control, but he explained that you need to bargain from strength. This became one of the leading themes of the Reagan administration, and he claimed in the end to be clearly vindicated.

In the early stages he wanted to delay arms control negotiations until the buildup had been put into place. This was the first aspect of the Reagan presidency to be revised. It was the first sign of a significant change. In that same year he adopted Carter's dual track strategy of negotiating on arms control in Europe while continuing to carry out plans for deploying new weapons, the Pershing II and the ground-launched cruise missiles. This too was soon to change.

Speaking to the National Press Club in November 1981, he announced his famous "zero-option," calling for the elimination of intermediate-range missiles on both sides.   This concept was destined to become the centerpiece of his foreign policy achievement.   When the speech was made, many considered it essentially a propaganda ploy and not a serious proposal. They felt that Reagan presumed the Russians would reject it. Reagan seized the opportunity because he knew his formula would make for a good speech and would be an effective reply to Soviet propaganda in Western Europe. The Reagan administration had encountered a great deal of trouble early in 1981. Ill-advised remarks by both Reagan and Haig had helped ignite the nuclear freeze and the peace movements in both Europe and the United States. Haig talked about a nuclear demonstration, that is, a warning shot across the bow, thereby alarming many Europeans. Reagan in a rambling discourse made some unfortunate remarks about how the United States might limit a nuclear exchange, implying that maybe he thought limited nuclear war was feasible. It was in the course of responding to the public alarm caused by these statements that the zero-option was put forward, and it proved initially to be remarkably effective.

Much of the benefit of the early propaganda was short-lived, because Reagan continued to hew a very hard line in his rhetoric toward the Soviets. But at least he launched the zero-option proposal, and in the same speech he called for the inaugurating of the Strategic Arms Reduction Talks (START). He had consistently criticized the arms control efforts of the 1970s for allowing a continued buildup of nuclear forces. He wanted reductions, and he positioned himself skillfully in that respect.   Nevertheless, he adhered to a very hard-line, and it was in 1983 that he made the famous speech in which he said that the Soviets were "the focus of evil in the modern world." Possibly at the end of 1983, if you were prescient, you could see the change coming. Clearly by 1984 the change had occurred, and there was a definite softening of tone in the speeches that he gave beginning in January 1984.

Obviously in an election year, he was sensitive to criticism regarding his hard-line stance, the delay in arms control negotiations, the lack of progress and the fact that there hadn't been a summit conference. In looking back to the election of 1980, we note that Reagan trailed Jimmy Carter only on the closely related questions of peace, fear of war, and arms control; those were the same issues on which the President was vulnerable in the 1984 competition with the Democrats. Perhaps Reagan adjusted his position primarily for that reason, but he was also adjusting to a persistent aspect of American opinion. The American public since the end of World War II has mixed its anti-Soviet animosity with a deep longing for reassuring signs of peace. Reagan had to find a position that would enable him to continue with his military buildup and the maintenance of a firm line toward the Soviets, but one that would also reassure both European and American opinion that he was effectively going to maintain the peace.

Thus we got that very important speech of 16 January 1984, in which Reagan set the tone for his second term by talking about three guiding principles: realism, strength, and dialogue. In dealing with the issue of change and consistency, I want to mention that while his speech reflected a significant change, one of the remarkable things about Reagan is that he had positioned himself very shrewdly in ways that allowed him to maneuver to take advantage of changing circumstances. When he had launched his call for a military buildup and the need for strength, he was careful to mention the importance of negotiation. Even in his inaugural address, he had said in regard to peace, "We'll negotiate for it, sacrifice for it," and so on. In his interview with Cronkite he had made it clear that he wasn't ruling out a summit meeting with Brezhnev. It was a false interpretation of his stand that he was not interested in negotiation.

Another thing that is remarkable about Reagan is that he embraced nostrums and made them politically viable. He is already famous for this.   The quintessential nostrum is supply-side economics. He was going to balance the budget in four years while having a military buildup and a tax cut. It's the kind of policy that his competitor in 1980, George Bush, called "voodoo economics." It led, as predicted, to massive federal deficits, but it also proved to be politically viable. It was winning politics, and Bush came around to that as a reality of domestic politics.   That's why, when he campaigned successfully for the presidency in 1988, he kept saying, "Read my lips. No new taxes." Taxes had become the "T" word in the 1988 election.

The nostrum in foreign policy was the Strategic Defense Initiative (SDI), which some physicists criticize as being technologically impossible, ridiculous, counterproductive, and destabilizing. Nonetheless, Reagan made it viable policy. SDI was appealing because it seemed to put him on the side of doing something about nuclear arms. He expressed great concern; he was going to render nuclear weapons impotent and obsolete. It also appealed to Americans who like technological solutions to serious and complicated problems.

For those who questioned his vision of an astrodome-like protection, there was the possibility that it might be feasible for protecting land-based missiles in case of a first strike. Thus, it might even have some military utility. When critics complained about the expense, Reagan would just shrug and say that it's a research program now and we'll see if it works. All of the problems of escalating costs or of destabilizing the arms race would be shoved on to successive administrations. It wasn't going to disrupt the politics of his own terms as President. Finally, Reagan's supporters can make a cogent argument that it put pressure on the Soviets, who genuinely feared the SDI program. Some even claimed that it was a major factor in bringing the Soviet Union back to the negotiating table.

Another tremendous asset for Reagan was his optimism. I think that's one reason he could embrace nostrums. He believed there was going to be a happy ending. People would talk about complications, but he had an abiding faith that it would turn out all right. I guess you have to combine that with Reagan's "luck of the Irish" in explaining how, contrary to many predictions, many things did basically turn out all right.

I want to make a couple of observations about Reagan's skillful positioning. Reagan usually put himself in a position where he could maneuver in various directions no matter what happened. When negotiations didn't go well on arms control, he could blame the Soviets. For example, when he deployed the Pershing II and cruise missiles and the Soviets walked out of negotiations, he simply said the negotiations were failing because the Soviets refused to talk. When they returned to the negotiating table in January 1985, he reiterated the virtues of patience and of negotiating from strength. When Gorbachev increased public pressure for an agreement by making concessions, Reagan could cooperate in reaching an agreement and then claim vindication for his policies.

Another important aspect about Reagan is that his actions often didn't match his hard-line rhetoric. This is one of the things that enabled him to succeed. In some respects his policies were even softer than his predecessor's. He fulfilled his campaign promise to dismantle Carter's grain embargo that had been instituted after the invasion of Afghanistan. His so-called sanctions against the Polish government for cracking down on Solidarity were mild and carefully measured. His response to the Soviet Union's shooting down of a Korean airliner was essentially rhetorical and minimal sanctions were instituted. He resorted to relatively strong measures to block the building of the Siberian pipeline to Europe, but he backed off from that after he got into trouble with NATO allies. He denounced the SALT II treaty as "fatally flawed," yet he abided by its provisions throughout his first term, and in the second term allowed only a token violation of that treaty.

After Gorbachev arrived on the scene and made far-reaching concessions, the negotiations followed a kind of zig-zag path. Although Reagan maintained his goal of eliminating intermediate-range missiles, he showed flexibility. He proposed modifying the zero-option with an interim approach that would temporarily allow the retention of some missiles in that class. That interim arrangement proved, of course, to be unnecessary. Agreeing to implement the zero option, Gorbachev and Reagan signed the Intermediate-range Nuclear Forces (INF) Treaty at the Washington summit in December 1987, and the Senate ratified it in time for the Moscow summit in the spring of 1988. By then Reagan had transformed his record on the so-called "peace issues." He had held more summits than any other president. He had negotiated the first treaty that actually eliminated a class of weapons. He was on a roll by the summer of 1988 and was able to claim this as substantive proof that his principles were vindicated.

What was Reagan's legacy? A journalistic cliche that emerged after the summit was that Reagan had virtually institutionalized top-level meetings of Soviet and U.S. leaders by making them seem normal and routine. Actually, Reagan's achievement went well beyond this. He developed a political position that enabled him to negotiate with the Soviets without opening himself to the kind of damaging criticism that disrupted the detente policy of Nixon, Ford and Kissinger. Detente of the early and mid-1970s was vulnerable to criticism on four points. First, it was oversold. Nixon and Kissinger had taken a thrashing for raising expectations too high on detente. Secondly, it slighted key American values such as human rights. Carter was able to beat up on Ford, Kissinger, and Nixon on this issue. After Solzhenitsyn wasn't invited to the White House, Carter developed a very effective campaign theme about the place of human rights in American foreign policy. Thirdly, detente seemed to reflect U.S. decline, and finally, it did not restrain Soviet expansionism in the Third World.

Reagan's handling of Soviet-American relations, despite all of its shortcomings, effectively protected his negotiations and agreements from all of these criticisms. First, by making his suspicion of the Soviet system axiomatic, he was always well positioned to explain any subsequent intensification of Soviet-American antagonism or Soviet acts of bad faith. Furthermore, while some of his judgments about Gorbachev struck critics, especially those on his right wing, as alarmingly naive, he dealt with them effectively. When asked about his early speeches in which he said Soviet leaders embraced lying, cheating, and so on in promoting world communism, Reagan said simply that Gorbachev was different.

Moreover, his comments focused only on Gorbachev and implied no support for the Soviet system. Nor could Reagan's simplistic but not entirely inaccurate statement that Gorbachev was different outweigh a long career of Soviet bashing. Indeed, Reagan's apparent intensification of the Cold War during his first term established such low expectations for relations with the Soviets that when an improvement did finally occur, he appeared to have delivered more than was generally expected. Reagan's credentials as a cold warrior also protected him from charges of naivete, except from his right wing. Furthermore, his administration continued to stress the importance of readiness and vigilance. One aspect of this was a coordinated emphasis on candor. Thus, on his visit to the Soviet Union in August 1988, Frank Carlucci, who was national security adviser and later secretary of defense, asserted that the Soviets remained in an offensive military posture in spite of their highly publicized announcements that they were adopting a defensive strategy. You'll note that the Bush administration continued the same line this year [1989].

Reagan was even more careful to avoid any appearance of slighting human rights. In his pursuit of agreements with the Soviets, clearly his administration had not neglected the lesson of recent American political history. In 1974, Senator Henry Jackson won a sensational legislative victory on this issue when the Senate considered a Soviet-American trade agreement. He secured the Senate's approval for an amendment making most-favored-nation treatment contingent upon the liberalization of Jewish emigration. Subsequently, Jimmy Carter scored major gains by developing the theme of human rights. So potent was this issue in the mid-1970s, that it became, rhetorically at least, the centerpiece of Carter's foreign policy. Although Reagan adopted Jeane Kirkpatrick's views to criticize Carter's human rights policies for their alleged weakening of American allies, he did not hesitate to denounce Soviet oppression. Indeed, to make himself impregnable on this issue, he spoke forcefully about human rights during a stopover in Helsinki while en route to the Moscow summit. Furthermore, while in Moscow he deliberately dramatized the point that negotiating with the Kremlin did not mean a retreat on human rights. Risking the displeasure of his host, he made remarkably frank public statements and even more notably held highly publicized meetings with Russian dissidents and religious leaders. Fortunately for Reagan, Gorbachev's reactions were far milder than the abuse that his predecessors heaped upon Carter for making similar gestures. Reagan did, incidentally, show some sensitivity to Gorbachev's embarrassment. While in Moscow, he attributed restrictions on Jewish emigration from Russia to a "bureaucratic bungle." Obviously it was more than a bureaucratic bungle, so Reagan left himself open to criticism, but overall he was very effective in making the point that he was keeping human rights prominently on the agenda.

At home the reactions of the public also lacked the negative undertones that surfaced during Carter's presidency. Reagan's theme in negotiating from strength effectively countered the earlier tendency to associate detente with U.S. decline. A *Washington Post* poll taken shortly after the Moscow summit indicated that Reagan got more credit for boosting America's morale than for American economic prosperity. His theme of standing tall proved to be enormously popular. Moreover, despite continuing scandals of waste, fraud, and abuse in the Pentagon, far more Americans thought that the United States became militarily stronger under Reagan than said it became weaker. The *Washington Post* survey also reported that 41 percent of those interviewed said U.S. influence in the world had increased, in contrast to only 24 percent who thought it had declined.

The hard-liners maintain the view that although the Soviet Union and its clients were in retreat from various Third World countries, we had to maintain an assertive and strong foreign policy. We needed to continue the military buildup and so on. They said that the vindication of this was the retreat by the Soviets in the Third World. The Reagan administration insisted upon making Soviet involvement in the Third World a prominent item on all the summit conference agendas, especially at the Washington and Moscow summits. In the aftermath of the Moscow summit the President seemed to be having his way: Soviet troops were leaving Afghanistan; the number of Vietnamese troops in Kampuchea was declining; an agreement in principle for a Cuban pullout from Angola was announced; and the Kremlin was obviously disenchanted with the fruits of its aid to Ethiopia. These developments not only marked a reversal of the situation from the late 1970s, when the Soviets appeared to be on the march in the Third World, but also seemed to vindicate the idea of linkage. Reagan revived the idea of linkage when he entered the White House, stubbornly insisting that the Soviets rein in their clients and cease foreign adventures.

While the discredited detente of the 1970s appeared to permit, if not invite, Soviet expansion, Reagan's agreements with the Soviets on arms control were linked to Soviet withdrawal. Moreover, the publicity given to the Reagan Doctrine in general, and the delivery of Stinger missiles to the Afghan rebels in particular, reinforced the notion that the new Soviet-American accommodation resulted to a significant extent from U.S. strength and firmness.

Since the superpowers seem to be entering a new era, many people are beginning to wonder what historical forces are at work and where they are going to take us. If we look back on the whole period of the Cold War, the fact that Cold War relationships may be in the process of being liquidated is not necessarily something to cheer about. It is generally applauded as a positive development, but I have doubts about that. We have lived through a halcyon period, and I believe that many beneficial effects came about as a result of American policy and extraordinary U.S. leadership during this period. In the future, however, with the breakdown of bipolarity and with what might be a decline in American global leadership, the world may not be such a safe and nice place to be. I think we have been living through a Long Peace in world history. Some of the best decades may have been the ones over which the U.S. presided.

Furthermore, I am not convinced that if Gorbachev succeeds in Russia the world will be a better place. This is no longer a new idea. When I wrote my piece, "Historical Reflections on the Dangers Ahead," for the *Virginia Quarterly Review* six years ago, Reagan was still in his hard-line phase and was talking about the need for capitalism around the world. He has claimed that he was vindicated, even in the communist world, by attempts to put free-market elements into the economies of China and the Soviet Union. However, we might face greater trouble if the Soviet Union were to develop a dynamic capitalist economy, because it is a very big and populous country, and would therefore be much tougher to deal with. The Russians have a very long history of expansionism.

There are also potentially serious dangers in continued Soviet retrenchment and decline. The Soviets have kept the lid on the Balkans. If quarreling rival nationalities set off wars in southeastern Europe, very dangerous tensions could be created in Europe.

The change in Soviet-American relations, furthermore, is going to give German nationalists and nationalism an opportunity for revival. Some people say this is nothing to worry about because the Germans are now prosperous and democratic. Yet one never knows; maybe the German role in starting World War I and World

War II should be regarded as a salutary warning of the dangers inherent in a revival of the German problem.

To be sure, recent events have reminded us of how difficult it is to predict the future. We don't know what will develop in the long run, but for now it appears that Ronald Reagan was extraordinarily successful in his policy toward the Soviet Union. Whether this was merely a matter of luck is another issue. Critics will stress the fortuitous factors within the Soviet Union that created this historic opening. Even acknowledging the validity of that view, historians should note, however, that Reagan at least had the flexibility—as he has always had—to seize opportunities. In carving out a place for himself in history, he was willing to embrace the idea of negotiating with the Soviet Union, and he did so in a way that maintained a foreign policy consensus, unlike his predecessors. He may have been lucky, but he is still in a position to claim that he was vindicated.

The final piece of Reagan's luck may be that perestroika will fail. We'll have to wait and see about that.

QUESTION: To what extent did the decisions, the speeches, the policy implementation and articulation result from collegial activity and how much from native shrewdness on the part of Mr. Reagan himself?

MR. KERNEK: On your point about native shrewdness, I think that during Reagan's long political career—especially if you include the years of the 1960s when he was on the "mashed-potato" circuit making a lot of political speeches—he developed an intuition of what would fly with the American peopl̤. He was perceptive about that. For example, one can look at the invasion of Grenada in which Reagan wanted a victory over communism. He wanted a roll-back kind of victory, and Grenada was a safe and easy target. It fit his innate criteria for not taking really big gambles. He talked big, but didn't take big gambles in action. Some media commentators initially were very skeptical as to how people would react to the invasion. Reagan, however, knew how they would react from the beginning. He knew that it would be applauded and that it would go over very successfully. The whole issue was sealed as soon as that student got off the plane in the United States and kissed the ground. Reagan's intuition on how the American people would react was often very good. I think that it was the product of many years of experience in getting feedback from his speeches.

Reagan also has a native intuition for maintaining some flexibility in his stances; he was willing to maneuver. If he was told by his aides that a policy was going sour, he was willing in most instances to back off from it. In that sense, he was the kind of chief executive who could function if he got reasonably good work from his staff. He did not have the ability to process policy options in the way that Jimmy Carter did. He was an intuitive thinker; unlike Carter, who could diagram a lot of his decisions, he wouldn't reason things out in ways that could be diagrammed.

On the matter of collegiality I've had mixed reports. Some people say that all the members in the Cabinet would be heard at a meeting. From reading memoirs and "kiss-and-tell" books, one gets the sense that policy-making was not an orderly process during the Reagan administration. We know that different department chiefs were vying with one another, and that another tactic for influencing policy was to try to insert a policy into a speech that the President was to deliver.

COMMENT: Several speakers have expressed the highest regard for Reagan as a person while they have been less than enthusiastic about some of the things he did during his two terms. He seemed to command enormous respect and loyalty. How does this fit with what you have said about his instinct and intuition?

MR. KERNEK: Maybe I haven't researched this deeply enough to see the common thread, but there again the reports seem contradictory. Some insiders say that he really didn't engender a warm sense of loyalty. He didn't seem to be interested in the intimate details of his staff's welfare. On the other hand, he has often been spoken of in respectful terms by people who are very able judges of leaders. There are flaws in the man. If he had really engendered deep loyalty, I don't think we would have seen such a spate of "kiss-and-tell" books while he was still in office.

I have some doubts about some of his personal qualities, but as a leader he had what James Nathan calls a "natural grace." When he was shot, he could joke with the surgeons. He was very gracious towards the opposition. He was capable of nice gestures when there were national tragedies. No one could preside at a funeral better than Ronald Reagan. His ability to make a speech was unparalleled. One denigrates the man by suggesting that he would select a foreign policy issue on the basis of whether or not it would make a good speech, yet I think there is an element of truth in that. On the other hand, Jimmy Carter couldn't make a good speech, and that was one of the flaws in his leadership. Effective speaking—especially on television—is a powerful tool in a democratic society.

QUESTION: There were some writers who felt that Reagan's change in attitude towards the Russians was influenced by his wife. They suggest that she thought if he were to have a place in history, he would have to abandon his hard-line policy. Do you agree with that?

MR. KERNEK: Yes, I think that is true. She was a very important person in his life. If she embraced that idea, he would have considered it seriously. I also think, however, that he would have done it even if she hadn't been there. What president doesn't want a favorable place in the history textbooks? The lowering of tensions with the Soviet Union was the high road to achieving that.

This gives me an opportunity to inject a point about Reagan's luck. While the Soviets were overextending themselves, Reagan railed about Soviet expansionism. Once they were overextended, the Soviet authorities began to shift gears. Thus, around 1980—the same time that Reagan was sounding the alarm for a military buildup—the Soviets were entering a period of retrenchment. The timing was perfect. When Reagan put his policy of military buildup into place, the Soviets retrenched, and Reagan claimed credit for this retrenchment. Due in part to a deep economic crisis, we have had the advent of Gorbachev. The Soviets are now clearly changing direction, probably largely for internal reasons, yet Reagan can say that these changes again demonstrate that his principle of bargaining from strength works.

Even his policy of patience was ideal. His partner in this, Gorbachev, was dynamic and clever about public relations. Combine this with the economic crisis Gorbachev faced, and all one has to do is wait. Gorbachev would put something on the table and if the United States didn't agree with it, he would soon make a better offer. So patience worked beautifully. Reagan's policy had the ideal partner, and everything fell into place.

QUESTION: Why do you suppose linkage was not exerted in the area of maximum concern to America, that is, Soviet influence in Central America? Was there a reason why this was impractical? Certainly the Soviet withdrawal from Afghanistan and the withdrawal of Cuban troops from Angola were not nearly as significant to us as a withdrawal of Soviet influence from this hemisphere would be.

MR. KERNEK: One reason may be that it is harder to make linkage work in Central America because it is such an ace for the Soviets. The Soviets can cause so much aggravation so cheaply there that they are very reluctant to give up that leverage, as long as we're hurting them in Afghanistan. U.S. aid to the Afghan rebels hurts the Soviets; it's a humiliation.

Furthermore, we can't make linkage work in Central America. The United States can't invade Nicaragua because of the vestiges of the Vietnam syndrome, and because it would probably be stupid to do so anyway. I hope that the latter is the principal reason why the Reagan administration didn't do it.

COMMENT: It is important to the Soviets, therefore, to retain Central America as a bargaining tool; just as we like to have tools with which to bargain.

MR. KERNEK: I'm sure it's been raised as a matter of linkage but, of course, we haven't insisted on it. The administration applied linkage in a flexible way. They put it on the agenda, but they didn't make hard and fast demands. Certainly nothing was going to hold up the INF Treaty.

QUESTION: You made the point that if Gorbachev's reforms work, we might find ourselves in a difficult spot. Approximately a year ago, the journal *International Affairs* (London) said exactly the same thing about China, that we were a bit naive in pushing Deng's reforms. Are you saying that we are somewhat naive in supporting Soviet reforms?

MR. KERNEK: On balance, yes. The study of history doesn't enable you to make predictions with certainty because every historical situation is unique. It does raise warning flags, however, and when other power centers expand, they become potentially more threatening. On the other hand, they could be benign. You don't know; there may be generations of quiescence. After Bismarck united Germany in the 1860s, he remained in control of German foreign policy for a long time with no disastrous short-term consequences. His assumption was that Germany was satiated and that there would be big trouble in Europe if Germany tried to expand further. He was able to rein the Germans in, but after his dismissal in 1890, the Germans became more assertive, and this assertiveness became destabilizing. It could not have been destabilizing if the Germans didn't have that power. Similarly, if the Chinese and the Soviets develop more power, there is the potential that this will be destabilizing. If you look at the history of Russia, it is not very reassuring. The lesson of history seems to be that if the Russians have power, they will expand. It may be, however, that although they can adopt elements of capitalism, the assertion of nationalism within the individual republics will be a corresponding source of weakness. The threat of their growing power, therefore, may be neutralized.

QUESTION: Do you think that the United States is wrong in promoting a capitalist China and Russia?

MR. KERNEK: I would say that it worries me in the long run. Capitalism is a better system than communism, but I would rather have them remain weak. To the extent that capitalism promotes strength, it's going to be a potential source of worry.

COMMENT: Your analysis is based on the assumption that there is never going to be any change in human behavior. According to you, it would seem, there is nothing to be gained from studying the world situation and studying societies, because the Russians cannot change. Gorbachev, however, is of a new generation.

There is an element of hope that people are striving for an improvement in society. It's not simply political antagonism. I think that Reagan benefitted by the forces that were being generated for change within the Soviet Union. The fact that

Reagan started out with the hard-line did not discourage Gorbachev because it was what he expected. This was the reaction to the former Soviet posture of expansionism. So he was able to change without any problem because he was a part of a receptive group. I think we have overlooked the human element.

MR. KERNEK: I understand what you are saying, but it is a political process. I agree that Reagan was the perfect partner for Gorbachev, and Gorbachev for Reagan. I also agree that what Reagan did in his first term vindicated Gorbachev's arguments that Brezhnev's policies were provoking a U.S. buildup, leading to Soviet overextension, and causing the economy to stagnate. There is a new wind blowing in the Soviet Union. I mentioned Reagan's conviction that Gorbachev is different, and I think he is fundamentally right about that. It is a question of whether or not what you are calling the human element could prevent a return to Soviet expansionism.

COMMENT: I would think so, because if it penetrates the ruling class, certainly there is going to be some effect on the general course of foreign relations.

QUESTION: In your analysis of Reagan you have followed the general assessment of Donald Regan, who says that the members of the right wing in the Republican party who thought that Reagan was their man were always wrong. Regan says that Reagan was always moderate. I think that in the first administration it was the members of the right wing who commanded the most attention, people like Richard Pipes, Richard Allen, Fred Iklé and Richard Perle. But it certainly was never a monolithic administration. There are simply too many people in any administration to have them all think the same way. As he moved forward toward accommodation with Russia, Reagan was moving in ways not far from his own convictions.

That still leaves unanswered this basic question as to whether Reagan, as he moved in this new direction, was his own man, or whether he was still a "hands off" president. Was he directed by those gaining his attention? Did the moderates, including his wife, Michael Deaver, and others gradually push the right wing away, and gain control of his mind and policy because they could convince him that there was greater diplomatic and political mileage to be found in a softer stance? You seem to make the suggestion that Reagan was his own man rather than being part of a group.

MR. KERNEK: A man as ill-informed about details as Reagan has to be part of a group, part of an administration, to succeed. He has to have a good staff around him or he is out of it. That's the reality of the Reagan presidency. On some things, however, he cares deeply. Within a narrow range, he is an activist, and he wants to preside over events. One thing about Reagan is that he maneuvers into a position where he is presiding in the limelight. He made it clear on certain issues that he wanted certain things, and forceful people in his administration had to accept that. When he decided he wanted an INF treaty, he was going to get it. He was in charge on that issue.

It is definitely true that he was not understood by the right wing. Responding to critics of the INF Treaty from the right wing, he said, "Some of the people who are objecting the most and refusing to accede to the idea of ever getting any understanding basically, down in their deepest thoughts, have accepted that war is inevitable whether they realize it or not." This was not a new idea for Reagan. During the first year of his administration he asserted, "I have always recognized that ultimately there has got to be a settlement, a solution." He always believed that eventually we had to get together with the Soviets. He said, "If you don't believe that, then you are going to find that in the back of your mind you accept that the inevitability of conflict is going to end the world." This remark suggests a long-perceived fundamental difference that he saw between himself and some of his hard-line supporters. He articulated it in the first year of his administration and it cropped up at the end of the administration. I wouldn't want to put myself in Don Regan's camp generally, but on that issue I agree with him.

NARRATOR: Mr. Kernek has been as insightful and helpful on this visit to the Miller Center as he was on his first visit. Thank you very much.

Mr. Kernek received valuable assistance from Mr. William D. Anderson with data and information for this article.

CHAPTER 2

REAGAN AND THE REALITIES
OF FOREIGN POLICY*

PAUL H. NITZE

NARRATOR: James Reston has written that perhaps no public servant has had a more constructive impact on the making and implementation of American foreign policy than Paul H. Nitze. Mr. Nitze served in the Truman administration State Department as the director of the Policy Planning Staff. He played a major role in the Johnson administration as assistant secretary for international security affairs in the Department of Defense and then as secretary of the Navy. He was involved in the SALT I negotiations during the Nixon administration. He later became the head of the negotiating team in Geneva for the Reagan administration. Following that, he was special assistant and adviser on arms control to President Reagan and Secretary George Shultz. That role is one that historians will be discussing for a long time to come. In the pages that follow, Mr. Nitze offers an insider's perspective of the Reagan administration and its foreign policy.

MR. NITZE: I want first to address the question of the Reagan administration and my impressions of that administration. I hadn't known Mr. Reagan at all until his campaign for the Republican nomination in 1980. At that time, before he had been nominated, Mr. Reagan came to Washington and stayed at the Mayflower Hotel a number of times; while there he would ask people to come and see him in his suite. I think the first time I saw him he had

---

Presented in a Forum at the Miller Center on 23 October 1989.

asked Gene Rostow, Jeane Kirkpatrick, General Edward Rowny, and me to consult with him, which we did. It was a rather mixed bag, for Rowny and I didn't agree, and Jeane Kirkpatrick didn't agree with the two of us; Rowny was off on one slant, and Rostow was off on another; he was primarily interested in Israel and the Middle East.

I later got a telephone call from Mr. Reagan's office saying that he wanted to have a completely off-the-record meeting with me and asked how that could be arranged. I said that wasn't any problem at all. I invited him to come and have dinner alone with me at my house. Phyllis, my wife, had agreed to this, but then it turned out that Mr. Reagan wanted to bring two of his advisers, Michael Deaver and Edwin Meese, as well as Eugene Rostow. The five of us had dinner together. It actually was a fabulous evening. He wanted Gene and me to brief him on national security and arms control policy. As I remember it, Gene and I were in pretty good voice; we rather dominated the conversation. Mr. Reagan was impressed because he really didn't know much about the national security situation at that time; he really didn't.

Later I was asked to go to California after he had been nominated, and I worked with him there. At that stage of the game, I was becoming confirmed in my mind that Mr. Reagan really didn't know that much about foreign or national security policy. He had a press and public affairs adviser—who later got into trouble in some way or other—who seemed to be the most sensible of the whole lot. The most ridiculous fellow, I thought, was his adviser on economics. I forget his name, but he was an advocate of supply-side economics, which I thought was a wilderness.

NARRATOR: Arthur Laffer or Martin Anderson?

MR. NITZE: Both. At that stage of the game, I was not very confident about Mr. Reagan.

However, toward the end of his administration I developed quite a different view of Mr. Reagan. I began to believe that although he might have all kinds of defects—not having mastery of the details, and not having a very good sense of organization or of the selection of people—the one thing that was clear was his absolutely firm conviction on the superiority of the democratic free system over a totalitarian system. He was prepared to speak up eloquently on this, and he was a very good spokesman for that point of view; he was helped in this regard by a very good speech writer by the name of Tony Dolan, who I felt was first class. Mr. Reagan stuck to this major issue, the superiority of a free system to a totalitarian system, and he did it with complete conviction; there was no doubt in his mind about it. His message was always well expressed, and he clearly won the debate on that issue with Gorbachev at the last summit in Moscow; he won hands down on the major issue.

If you have a presidential spokesman who can win an international debate of that kind and win it hands down, you can't help but have a high regard for him. My view is that he should go down in history as a very superior president on the main issue; the main issue was eloquently defending the value system of the United States. Mr. Reagan did so against all comers, carrying that message to the world.

QUESTION: As a retired general, I have doubts about our military spending priorities. I wonder why we need both B-1 and B-2 bombers in the Air Force; I think B-52s have been quite sufficient for a number of years. I wonder why we need four battleships. I wonder why we need backup numbers of army divisions to go somewhere, when they couldn't get there if they had to go. From your perspective, having tried to arbitrate military spending and priorities, what would be your recommendation?

MR. NITZE: I find simple answers to all these various questions difficult. The contingencies that you run into are different from the ones you plan for; I think we need a balanced capability to do things that are often unforeseeable. The main point here is that if you look at the possibility of our having to intervene with conventional forces in the Middle East, the Far East, or some such place, the capabilities you need under those circumstances are quite different from the basic ones you need in the event of a nuclear war. Those contingencies that are short of nuclear war may be politically the most important ones, however.

To take one example, I think the most difficult weapon system to defend, perhaps, is the battleship. If you look at their survivability, it would take about 20 direct hits to sink a battleship; it takes somewhat less to disable it. However, you care not only whether or not it is going to sink; you care what the enemy will have to put into it in order to counter a battleship. In addition, when you want to get pinpoint destruction on the shore, a battleship is a very superior beast. Then you ask yourself whether it is worth the cost. My conclusion was that it was worth the incremental cost of keeping it in commission.

When you go through the other items that you mentioned, the analysis for some of them is more difficult. Of course, the capability is quite different between the B-1 and B-2. If the B-2 actually does work the way it is supposed to work, it would be very hard to shoot down because it is so difficult to locate. It isn't that you can't see the thing, but a radar can't see it with sufficient accuracy for a fire-control system to shoot it down. Thus, it has virtues that the B-1 doesn't have. Is it worth the billions that have gone into it? That isn't the question any more. I think $14 billion have been spent on it. Would you advocate canceling it now, or do you want to get some value out of the $14 billion that we have put into it? Somebody who has gone into the benefits and incremental cost in greater detail than I have done will have to make those judgments.

QUESTION: What is your impression of the outcome of negotiations between the United States and the Soviets under Reagan and Gorbachev? Do you think they are going to work?

MR. NITZE: It depends what one means by "work."

COMMENT: I would call "work" resulting in continued peace.

MR. NITZE: I don't know that one can count on that. I would phrase it a different way. It seemed to me that the decisions that Mr. Truman made to go to the aid of Greece and Turkey in February 1947 when the British backed out of supporting Greece and Turkey were crucial to everything that has happened since. The heart of the matter arose in the period when George Kennan was advocating a policy of containment. The theory was that if you could contain Soviet or Stalinesque expansionism for a period of time, then eventually the Soviets would look inward, wouldn't like what they saw, and would try to change their system. I think that has happened, and is really the essence of what Gorbachev's shift in policy is all about. As a result, I believe the dangers of nuclear weapons have diminished.

Gorbachev once told us that before he became general secretary of the Communist party, he and Ryzhkov, who were both members of the Politburo under Andropov, had talked together about what the problems were in the U.S.S.R. and decided that they were manifold. They appointed a hundred study teams made up of what he called the best and brightest people they could tap. They came up with a whole series of reports which included the recommendations for glasnost and for perestroika and for a new look with respect to defense doctrine and policy. The way he put it was, "I didn't begin from a standing start when I became general secretary." They used those hundred reports, they put them together and decided how they were going to organize their campaign from that point on. That has been the basis for Gorbachev's policy, and it did fulfill what we were trying to do based on the doctrine of containment, the Greek-Turkish aid program, and all the myriad of policies and subpolicies that were decided on in 1947-48. We did persist in them, and they did bring about what we hoped they would. It took us somewhat longer than we had anticipated.

The amazing thing is the persistence of the American people in supporting something that was really very costly and dangerous—it was costly not only in monetary terms, but in human casualties. They persisted in doing this for 40 years, and that is the extraordinary thing that brought about the changes that Mr. Gorbachev has been masterminding.

The next question is: Will they work? I don't think they necessarily will, but the Soviets will be different. The threat from the Soviet Union will not be the same. Their objective had been to create a communist world; they are not going to be able to do that. They don't have the same assets that they could command before.

QUESTION: I'd like to ask you what your views are on the prospects for spending much less of our gross national product on so-called defense and turning it to other more urgent domestic problems. My feeling is that the real threat to this country at the moment is not a nuclear war or invasion of Europe by Russia, but various internal matters. What is the danger in letting our defenses down with this kind of thinking?

MR. NITZE: I think the dangers of letting it down would be very great indeed, but that isn't to say that the threat hasn't changed; I think it has changed. I think the main thing for which we should strive—and we can achieve this—is to try to get stabilizing reductions with the Soviet Union. They have as many as 40,000 nuclear weapons over there on the territory of the U.S.S.R., but who will control those weapons is uncertain. It is very much in our interest that they be controlled by someone who has some sense. It would be very dangerous for us and for the rest of the world if irresponsible people were to control those weapons. Accordingly, we can't just forget about the U.S.S.R. We have to deal with this problem more intelligently than in the past.

What kind of assets do we need? One of the important assets is to have a military capability that serves as a high-confidence deterrent, which isn't a cheap thing to do. You have to work at it. I am very worried about it, but that doesn't mean there aren't a lot of other things to worry about. The problem is that we have a lot of difficult problems in front of us; how we sort them out and deal with each one in a sensible way is not an easy task.

However, the policy option that everyone thinks is the obvious answer—just to cut the defense budget—I don't believe is right. It is going to be cut—there's no doubt about that—and we are going to withdraw some forces from Europe; but to withdraw a large number of them could have repercussions that we would subsequently regret very deeply.

QUESTION: I have two questions that aren't necessarily related. Why can't we or don't we have an array of giant radar stations, like the Soviets have, which is permitted, I assume, under the ABM Treaty (Antiballistic Missile Treaty) and could give us the earliest possible warning in case of a surprise attack?

Second, given the Soviet history of 70 years of a government dominated by a policy of secrecy and a doctrine that justified anything in the interests of communism, can we really proceed simply on the basis of trust, even with Gorbachev, no matter how reasonable and Western-like he may appear?

MR. NITZE: With respect to the first question, I take it you are talking about the powerful early warning radars they are building all over the U.S.S.R. I believe they are permitted by the ABM Treaty.

The only bar that the treaty puts on them is that they must be on the periphery of the U.S.S.R., be outward oriented, and must not be defended so that they could be destroyed early in any possible engagement.

The trouble with the Krasnoyarsk radar was that it was not on the periphery and not outward facing, and so it is a clear violation of the treaty. I think Mr. Gorbachev has come around to the view that the radar station should be dismantled, realizing that it has violated the treaty for a long period of time. They should get rid of it, and I think now they will.

Should we build radars that are permitted and of the same capability? I think it is more important to have satellites, which would give you the same information that these ground-based radars will, but I think more reliably. That's the way we have been headed in the past, and I think it is the correct way, backed up by some ground-based radars. You don't want to put all your eggs in one basket. I think we are doing that part of it all right. Consequently, I have higher confidence in our ability to detect an attack now than I would have had 10 or 20 years ago. I think this is one of the few places in which we have improved in our capabilities vis-à-vis the U.S.S.R.

In response to the second part of your question, Soviet party doctrine calls for deception in everything they do. It is not only a doctrine of misleading you, but of positively doing things to deceive you. For instance, all their maps were incorrectly drawn in order to deceive us in the event of a war. But they deceive themselves too. That has been their doctrine, and I don't believe it is totally extinguished. If you have been trained for generation after generation, you look at things that way; it is hard to get either 290 million people, the Politburo, or the million members of the *nomenclatura*, and all their close assistants to look at it differently.

Thus, I would be suspicious about what the Soviets tell us and what Mr. Gorbachev tells us. I disapprove of the extent to which the executive branch takes a view that all but declares that Gorbachev is our man and that we are going to defend him against his domestic enemies.

It reminds me of the days when many in the United States were so enamored of Chiang Kai-shek that it completely queered our objective view of the policy toward China. It also reminds me of when we were so enamored of the Shah in Iran that we were lying down like a dog on the floor trying to do everything for him; that was a very dangerous and stupid thing to do. We shouldn't get that personally involved with the leader of a foreign country; it gets us involved in their internal politics, and I think internal politics turn out differently than we anticipate, leaving us often on the wrong side of those issues sooner or later.

I do not think that we ought to simply accept Gorbachev at his word and try to defend him against all enemies. I think we ought to maintain a position of reserve and try to help him with constructive developments, but also keep our guard up in case these things change. You can't tell how they might change; you have to look at all the various contingencies and not let personal affection and emotions guide your policy.

QUESTION: I wonder if we could return to President Reagan for a moment and have you give us some picture of his relationship to the arms negotiation process. Did he change over the eight years, and if so, how? Was he sometimes close to the process and sometimes distant?

MR. NITZE: My view was that he started out with certain fixed ideas in his mind, and these were very difficult for anybody to get out of his mind. The first time I had a long discussion with him about arms control, he emphasized one thing above all others, that the Soviet Union and its leaders justifiably considered themselves encircled. I was never able to get that idea out of his mind. I kept reminding him about who was encircling whom, who did what to whom, and so forth. If you look into history, it was the Russians, whether under communist leadership or czarist leadership, who were the ones who expanded and expanded and expanded, and were one of the main participants in causing wars for several hundred years. It wasn't just the poor Russians feeling themselves surrounded. Their policy was one of expansionism. Certainly that was true of Stalin, and none of his successors would have abandoned that; it was part of Leninist doctrine. I thought Mr. Reagan was just wrong about the idea that Soviet leaders were justified in considering themselves to be surrounded. Others also considered themselves to be surrounded. In fact, more nations justifiably considered themselves to be threatened by the Soviet

Union than the Soviet Union could justifiably consider itself to be threatened by.

He also had the view that somehow or other nuclear weapons should be eliminated, which I thought was correct in a way—certainly politically correct. However, if you were going to do that, you would want to be sure that the process went through certain phases in order to get ready for it. You couldn't do it all at once.

The questions that arose in this process were ones such as what those phases should be, and how you could do it in a secure way. But there was also a question of the degree to which you wanted to get rid of nuclear weapons. If you go down to zero nuclear weapons, then any one person or any one country that develops a few is in a commanding position. Thus, wouldn't it be safer for everyone involved if there was a certain minimal fixed number? We spent a lot of time going through that, and we had come to the conclusion that maybe 500 to 1,000 was the right number on both sides, provided they were of a size such that they couldn't be MIRVed, and deployed in such a way that they weren't vulnerable to an initial strike, and it would take several weapons to take one out. The result would be inherently stable; even if someone were to come up with 200 or 300 weapons, it wouldn't be enough to change the balance. Therefore, there was some minimum number for which you ought to strive. I think many of the Russian analysts have recently come to the same conclusion; some say around 500 to 1,000 of the correct types and correctly deployed on each side would be much more stable and would guarantee much less danger of a war than smaller numbers. I think that is correct. Perhaps someone could persuade me otherwise, but I don't see a different answer to it yet.

QUESTION: Obviously the work of negotiation in arms control is one of the most important parts of our national effort. On the other hand, there is an apparent turnover of people once every three or four years. Is a deliberate effort being made to ensure continuity at least in some body of the organization, or do we have to have a new group of people come in and learn the game the hard way each time we have a turnover?

MR. NITZE: Obviously having been in this business for longer than anybody can remember, I think there is some merit in having people who have been in the business for a long period of time.

COMMENT: That's my concern, that we should have the ability to keep experienced people involved in the effort.

MR. NITZE: I think that's right, but we have transitions from one administration to another, and then we get into all the processes that are involved in how you have the best possible transition. We tackled that first, I guess, at the time of the transition from the Truman regime to the Eisenhower regime. Some of my people on the Policy Planning Staff and I addressed that specific question. Because early on it was pretty clear that Mr. Eisenhower was going to be elected, we had a lot of time to plan that transition. We developed what was called the black book, which outlined how the administration should proceed. We thought the important thing was to have Mr. Truman ask General Eisenhower to come and see him a day or two after the election and talk to him about the process of transition from the Truman regime to the Eisenhower regime. The hope was that, if planned in advance, it could be done more intelligently than it would otherwise have been done.

We wrote out the initial speech for Mr. Truman, and then we wrote out how we thought General Eisenhower would respond. That was phase two of this book; I imagined these two exchanges, and we wrote a third section anticipating what Mr. Truman's response would be. We didn't presume to imagine the very end of the discussion, however.

It went just the way that the black book had called for. Mr. Truman used it, and General Eisenhower did respond the way we had anticipated, and Mr. Truman's response was perfectly all right. General Eisenhower was not contrary, and so it was very successful.

We were trying to establish that it would be wise if Mr. Eisenhower appointed at least two people to represent his incoming administration during the transition period and work with the requisite people in the Truman administration through 20 January. We recommended that one should be a man familiar with the Bureau of the Budget problems and another should be a man familiar with international security items.

All that did work out, and Henry Cabot Lodge was chosen by the President-elect to represent the national security part of the exercise. Cabot Lodge came in to see us in the Policy Planning Staff the next day because we were appointed to be the liaison with him. We had a good two- or three-hour discussion with him, and then the following day, General Eisenhower decided that there was to be a big meeting aboard the cruiser *Helena* sailing in the Pacific in which the new administration was to work out its policies. Cabot Lodge didn't want to be excluded from that, so we never saw him again. Thus, that part of it was a total disaster. The budget part worked better. You can try, but you run into problems in working out a reasonable transition period.

QUESTION: It seems to me that Mr. Reagan's original SDI proposal was totally overstated and unrealistic in the way he presented it as an umbrella over the entire United States that would render nuclear weapons obsolete. What kind of scientific advice did he have before he made such a statement to the people of this country? What value have you found in the SDI proposal in your negotiations with the Soviet Union?

MR. NITZE: He had received advice from the science adviser at that time, George Keyworth. Others were marginally involved in providing that advice; Edward Teller was close to Keyworth, but he wasn't really the principal villain in this. One who was deeply involved was General Daniel Graham who had been head of Air Force Intelligence and who developed a program called "the high frontier." He was a general who had been twisting my arm to back him on the "high frontier" program, but I thought the analysis was not firm enough to warrant making this a key program.

In any case, the President was sold on this advice that I thought was of dubious scientific validity. One part of the program, of course, was to create two committees, one to look into the overall technical possibilities and the second one to look at a more detailed program. They did a lot of work and came up with a lot of interesting ideas, but as an outside observer, even though I had access to all the scientific work, I couldn't tell whether or not this had a chance of working.

My view was that the thing to do was to set some criteria that the system must have a good prospect of achieving before you went down the path of deploying such a system. Those criteria became known as the Nitze criteria. They stipulated that the system (1) should be effective, (2) should be able to defend itself against a direct attack, and (3) would be cost-effective at the margin—in other words, that you could increase your defense at less cost than that by which they could increase their offense against it, so that it wouldn't be in their interest to put more money in expanding their offense in order to defeat it.

Incidentally, these weren't my criteria. They were developed by some people in the Pentagon and then put into a speech by Admiral Watkins that appeared in the *Naval Institute Proceedings*. I had borrowed these ideas from him, but I think I put them more clearly and lucidly in a speech that I gave at Philadelphia. That's why they became known as the Nitze criteria. They were approved by the President and approved by the Congress so that they became law. Frankly, I still think they are right. I don't see any reason to change them.

The question was, could they be met by any foreseeable technology? I don't think anyone has developed a technology yet that can meet those criteria with a high degree of confidence. There are two different schemes that might meet it. One is the "brilliant pebbles" scheme, which depends upon miniaturization, bringing the necessary components down to a very small size. If that works, I think it would meet the Nitze criteria, but nobody knows yet whether it will work, and it is taking longer than had been expected to develop a test to see whether it would work or not. I don't foresee the rest of these ideas ever working, but it isn't yet totally foreclosed in my mind. However, I don't see any way today that you could have high hopes that they will work.

QUESTION: Has SDI had an influence on the negotiations with the Soviet Union?

MR. NITZE: I think so. The reason for that is not that their scientists have said that they see a prospect of its working and that they couldn't defeat it. Rather, the reason is that Mr. Gorbachev was impressed by the conviction that President Reagan had in it; Mr. Reagan was really convinced that this was going to work. Gorbachev couldn't imagine the President would be so convinced unless there was something about the program that he, Gorbachev, didn't know about. That may not be right, but that's what I believe.

QUESTION: Aren't the Soviets supposed to be working on an SDI equivalent?

MR. NITZE: They have been for years. I think their problem is in coming up with something that will really work.

QUESTION: Do we in this country realize that our diplomats do not come from a background anything like that of Soviet officials? Do we take into account where Mr. Gorbachev gets his information and how he weighs it?

MR. NITZE: I think in the past everybody has recognized the fact that Gorbachev is a convinced Leninist, and that he has been a master at tactics and a master at accumulating power for himself. One tries to figure out whether he has a strategy. I have come to the conclusion that he hasn't any strategy at all, if you define a strategy as not only having a panoply of objectives but also some reasonable course of action that you think might get you from where you are to where you want to be. He's got a lot of things that he thinks would be good, but he doesn't show any signs of having a course of action in mind that will get him from where he is to where he says he wants to be. Gorbachev is indeed a great tactician, which makes it possible for him to pull these totally unforeseeable coups out of his hat. Everybody else does what I do; we are thinking, "There's got to be a strategy; I can see what the strategy ought to be, and his next move ought to be this." However, he doesn't have a strategy, and consequently you can't foresee what his next move is going to be. Everybody else has been equally confused by this, particularly his opponents, so he takes them to the cleaners every so often and with regularity.

Now he has gotten the thing to a point where he is in fact a personal dictator, having established his position by the threat of putting people in the gulag. That's why, at the Supreme Soviet meeting—there were 4,000 of them there—all of them put up their hands saying "Yes," not knowing what the agenda was and not having access to any of the papers, but they all put up their hands in approval. You don't do that unless you know that doing the reverse is going to have serious consequences.

QUESTION: At least publicly, President Reagan often said, "Trust but verify." Do you see any likelihood that even with Gorbachev and an environment of greater openness, real verification will be any easier?

MR. NITZE: I think he is prepared to try, but some of these verification problems are inherently difficult. It isn't only the opposition of the Soviets. Take, for instance, chemical weapons. It is impossible to be sure that they are not being created in some backyard or bathtub or something like that. There the issue is a different one.

Suppose you permit chemical weapons to exist without any constraints; what are the risks then? If they are permitted by us, we have to make them because everyone else in the world will make them, and so on. What are the risks in that kind of an environment? I think you can make a pretty strong argument that the risks from cheating on an agreed ban are less, even though you know it is impossible to have high confidence in verification. I think the risks are less from cheating than they are from letting these weapons go unconstrained. You still want to do your best to ensure that you have the best chance possible to verify compliance, even when you don't have high confidence in them. It is a question of weighing some risks against other risks. Thus, I wouldn't consider verifications to be absolutely reliable.

Nuclear proliferation is another serious issue that indicates problems inherent in verification. What happens when verification has to be multilateral instead of merely bilateral? We have been riding herd on the Pakistanis, for instance, and they have not given us the information we require, and they have not done the things we think they should do in regard to their nuclear energy capabilities. We tried hard with the Indians to restrain them. With respect to the Chinese, they are not recognized as being a legitimate nuclear power. They've had nuclear weapons for so long that to get them within some kind of a tent you need some kind of general negotiations with many participants. Similarly, to arrive at an accord that would reduce strategic nuclear weapons more than 50 percent, you would need to include the Chinese, the Russians, ourselves, the British, and the French. The United States and Russia are prepared to try to achieve 50 percent reductions without the participation of any of the other nuclear powers, but for reductions below 50 percent, both countries agree that the participation in some way or other of the British, the French, and the Chinese is necessary. If you can get an agreement among those five, then you've got to ride herd upon the lesser powers: the Israelis, the Pakistanis, and the Indians, etc. I should think that's the way it is viewed by the great powers.

QUESTION: What is the cause of the changes in the Soviet Union?

MR. NITZE: My view is that the controlling factor has been the enormous percentage of their gross national product that they have been devoting to defense measures. I believe it is true that they themselves don't know what percentage of their gross national product goes to defense. At least that is what Gorbachev and others tell us, that they don't know how much is going into defense. Their books are so corrupt that you can't possibly tell. Looking from all the outside factors, I think that between 20 and 30 percent of their gross national product has been going into defense and things associated with defense. That compares with 6 percent or something like that for the United States. Thus, they are putting four or six times the percentage of GNP into defense than we have been putting in. We found it a burden, and they find it an impossible burden.

Therefore it is imperative that Mr. Gorbachev do what he is trying to do, to cut his defense expenditures in one way or another. Whether there are arms control agreements or not, he is going to have to cut his defense expenditures or he will never get out of his economic problems. That is my view of the matter.

We want to get agreements nailed down if possible in a way that is really beneficial to the rest of the world and to us, and that's what the administration is working on—to try to see whether that can be done. Now the Bush administration is putting a higher priority upon conventional force reductions in Europe, and I think quite logically, because that's where Mr. Gorbachev has to go. That's where most of the expenditures are for the Soviet Union and for us. For us, 80 percent is in conventional forces; for them it is less, perhaps 75 percent. However, they aren't really going to save enough money from cutting nuclear weapons. You get more bang for a buck with nuclear weapons than you do in conventional weapons, so it costs a lot more money to sustain big conventional forces. Thus, I think there is a real chance that it can be worked out. I know Mr. Gorbachev wants to do this.

Until this last year, I was very dubious that one could reduce conventional forces and verify it in a reliable way. It still is a very difficult proposition to do it in a verifiable way, no matter what Gorbachev wants to concede. It is inherently difficult, and there are all kinds of difficulties on the Western side. NATO is not of one mind about all the measures that are involved. To get an agreement in a way that not only could be agreed to but which could also be verified is probably not possible within the six-month deadline that the President has given. I would be amazed if it could be done in a rigorous way even in an additional six months. That doesn't mean to say that you couldn't figure out some series of agreements in which you agree in principle on this, that, and the other thing, but nothing is for keeps until you can work out the necessary verification models. It wouldn't be a solid agreement for some period of time, in my estimation. In the end, you have to work at it as hard as you can, and that's what I think the executive branch is trying to do.

QUESTION: How many of these changes do you think have been caused by the advancement of communications technology? They can no longer keep the people isolated from television, for instance.

MR. NITZE: Certainly that has an impact in Central Europe—in Poland, Czechoslovakia, and Hungary, where it is difficult for them to black out the television from Western Europe. It is harder for them to keep the type of secrecy that they kept before, and that does have an effect upon people, but so does the whole policy of glasnost.

It is hard to sort out what arises from the technical considerations when you have many people listening. I think it has played some role, but I would have thought the role of Gorbachev's policy decision to adopt glasnost played a greater part. I don't know how you weigh these various causes.

QUESTION: According to press reports, from time to time various European countries have expressed concern that we might be trading off their security in order to protect our own. Would you comment on the delicate balance that is required in negotiations on the subject of armament and the balancing of what is necessary to maintain European support, without at the same time weakening the bargain that we could possibly have if a different view were taken of our allies' interests?

MR. NITZE: It has been my view that there are two parts to the nuclear arms control negotiations. One part deals with the intermediate range and shorter range forces that are all stationed in Europe, where the primary and direct interest is on the part of the Europeans and where our interest is really secondary. Our interest derives from that of the Europeans and because of our forces stationed in Europe, which are there in part to deter an attack on the Europeans. With respect to those forces, it would seem to me, our prime interest was in the Europeans and how the Europeans saw them as contributing to their defense. The main purpose of those forces is for the defense of Europe.

With respect to the intermediate range force negotiations, for instance, in conducting the negotiations I saw myself as conducting them on behalf of the Europeans as much as on behalf of the United States. We never did anything in those negotiations without thoroughly consulting–really *consulting*, and not just informing–the Europeans. Between 1981 and 1988 I took some 82 trips to Europe consulting in various capitals. You had to do that because the essence of it was to have a consensus on the NATO side; otherwise the Russians weren't going to take you seriously and would try to break up the alliance. You had to have a unified alliance, and the allies had to know all about it before you did it, in order to make NATO policy work.

With respect to strategic forces, the intercontinental forces, there my quarrel has been that the Europeans never took them seriously enough. They have not been willing to understand that the whole of Western security depends upon the bottom line, our capability to deter strategic attack. If we were to lose the ability to deter strategic attack, the things we are doing in Europe would be worth nothing. This is the heart of the matter, and they don't realize that.

Thus, I am cross with the Europeans because they don't sympathize enough with us. They are dependent upon us for the bottom line, and yet they think we are doing this only for our own defense, which we have to do in any case; they don't appreciate that they too have an interest in it.

NARRATOR: Was the organization of the government for arms control negotiation in the Reagan administration about right? If you had changed it, how would you have done so? Did you have all the support and access you needed as a negotiator? How would you assess all this?

MR. NITZE: We had almost zero support as negotiators. I was very disappointed over the way in which the Washington government functioned in the INF negotiations from the very start. Part of the problem, to get personal about it, was the disagreement between Caspar Weinberger and George Shultz, and that of course had some structural origins, too.

The President didn't want to have anybody, short of himself, take a principal role as "vicar." (That came up in the case of Alexander Haig when he insisted that he was the vicar to the President. Haig claims he got it from me, and I firmly denied it because I've never used the word "vicar." I finally did see that it came from my testimony before the Jackson Committee, but that testimony was rewritten by C. B. Marshall. He changed the word "manager" to "vicar," which he rightly thought was more eloquent.) The President has never had, and never wanted to appoint, a vicar who would be his real deputy for arms control matters. The closest was Bill Clark, who was very close to the President. The President had very high regard for him. Bill was not in any way an expert in this field, but he was a very sensible person and he understood the President's point of view. I thought he handled the job better than anybody else has in the President's eight years in office. A lot of them were not very good.

Donald Regan was a disaster in my opinion, and some of the others as well. I was fond of Robert McFarlane and I thought very highly of him. He took his loyalty to the President too far, however, engaging in what I thought were unconstitutional acts in trying to defend the President from things he knew the President should take responsibility for. But I still thought well of McFarlane.

Concerning the others on the National Security Council, I had a high regard for Colin Powell, but the others were not, in my estimation, the right people to be supervising the national security work within the executive branch.

The difficulty within the executive branch was caused by a very simple problem, the completely different points of view of Shultz and Weinberger. Weinberger was inherently a litigator, and loved to litigate; when he was with Bechtel, Shultz told me he used to love to sue all their clients. Bechtel himself had to intervene and say, "We are in the construction business; we are not in the business of suing all our clients. Lay off." Similarly, within the executive branch, I think Weinberger had the view that the enemy was the Congress, principally the Democrats in the Congress. He had no conception of how an executive branch handles policy and its congressional relations in a period when the opposite party is in control of both the Senate and the House. It is an art, but it can be done.

If you look back to the period of 1947 when President Truman decided to stand up to the Russians, we were proposing a myriad of important and expensive programs, but both the Senate and the House were controlled by Republicans. Watching Mr. Acheson and General Marshall deal with that problem was a joy and a delight. There was a split in the Republican party between Senator Robert Taft and Senator Arthur Vandenburg. Senator Vandenburg had been only a second-rate senator, just handling in a second-rate way the special interests of the state of Michigan. However, after being reelected so often, he eventually came to the conclusion that he would get the necessary votes for reelection no matter what. Then the two of them—Marshall and Acheson—persuaded him that he had a great opportunity to become a statesman; he was all for that. They wrote the Vandenburg Resolution for him and did this, that, and the other in order to make him a statesman. There was then enough of a fight between Taft and Vandenburg that we could sail through the gap and get all our legislation passed, and that we did. It was a vast success, but it required some degree of astuteness as to how to handle a situation in which the other party controlled both houses of Congress.

I remember once telling this tale to Weinberger, just as I've told it to you, and Weinberger said, "This involves trying to build up somebody like Nunn," and I said, "Well, I think it does." He said,

"Nunn doesn't understand anything about defense; he's a complete disaster on the floor. I wouldn't think of having anything to do with Nunn." This made handling congressional relations in the Reagan administration an almost impossible task.

QUESTION: Could I ask how you view the importance of "two-track" diplomacy, talks between the two conflicting sides outside the formal negotiating table? I have in mind Jimmy Carter's trip to Camp David, as well as your "walk in the woods." Is there any way in which the whole process of confrontation can be softened effectively?

MR. NITZE: I think it is true that a point arises in every negotiation in which some other method, other than just confrontation between the two negotiating teams, has to be found in order to see whether you can find a possible solution in which both sides make concessions. Neither side wants to be caught in a position of having offered a concession without simultaneously assuring the concession that the other side has to make, and that is hard to do across the table in the course of a formal negotiation. Consequently, some other method has to be found. One method is to have it escalated to a higher level, and that's what Kissinger would do. He wouldn't keep any of us who were doing the negotiating at the table informed of what he was doing. That is not the right way to do it in my estimation; nor did he seek our advice, which I thought was a second error. Informal negotiations can be done at a higher level, but it is more dangerous because there is nobody to overrule the negotiator. At the presidential level it is virtually impossible to overrule what has been done.

It should be done, I think, at the same level as the negotiators sitting across the table, but it ought to be done without committing the government to the concessions that you are offering in recompense for the concessions that you are trying to get from them. It is a difficult and tricky kind of operation, but I think that at some time somebody has to do it.

QUESTION: Could you comment a bit on the military and political implications for U.S. power of the development of the European Community and of a unified Germany?

MR. NITZE: I consider that to be *the* current problem for our foreign policy. You can go through various aspects of it. I have spent a lot of time with the Germans recently. They feel that the restraints that were put upon them as a result of the lack of a peace treaty after the war are outdated, that they really should be relieved of those restraints, and that they are in a much better position to work with Poland, Hungary, Czechoslovakia, and even with the U.S.S.R. than anybody else in NATO. They feel they've managed to keep their budget balanced and produce these huge surpluses so that they have the economic capability, not only in terms of money but also in terms of people, to help all those areas better than anybody else has. They really are working at it. Outside of East Germany I think they are putting most of their effort into Poland at this time. They think it would be a tragedy if Poland were to deteriorate because they couldn't control their rampant inflation. It is going to take a large infusion of assets to do that, but I think it is worth it. The Germans are trying to do it themselves the best they can right now, but they want support from us and from the other NATO countries. It is not at all clear how big this liability will be and how much of that burden we should take. They think that is the crucial problem today in making the transition from a Communist state to a democratic state feasible, and if you can do it in one country then perhaps you can do it in others. It has to be tried with respect to Poland, and that is inherently a difficult thing to do. The Germans also look upon themselves as being in the best position to deal with the Hungarians and these other people whom I've discussed.

NARRATOR: We are delighted that Mr. Nitze has been with us. He is one of the great figures in American government and foreign policy, and we look forward to his further public service on behalf of the country. We hope he will visit us again.

CHAPTER 3

REAGAN AND
INTERNATIONAL ARMS AGREEMENTS*

An Interview With
CASPAR WEINBERGER

QUESTION: Secretary Weinberger, you met Ronald Reagan for the first time in 1965 during the California gubernatorial campaign. Did you have any expectations as you were meeting him? Did you have any contact with him during his union days?

MR. WEINBERGER: No, I had not met him before, I had not had any particular reason to have worked with him in his union days.

QUESTION: Had you committed to Mayor Christopher before the gubernatorial primary and then shifted?

MR. WEINBERGER: I had committed to Mr. Christopher before, and I stayed with my commitment. After Mayor Christopher was defeated in the primary by President Reagan, I, of course, supported the ticket. I had previously told President Reagan that if he won the primary I would support him, but that, unfortunately, I was tied up in a commitment I made before I knew he was entering the race.

QUESTION: If you had been a free agent, would you have supported Reagan?

*A phone interview with Caspar Weinberger on 21 August 1990.

MR. WEINBERGER: Without any question, yes.

QUESTION: What do you think of President Reagan's qualities as a leader?

MR. WEINBERGER: I think that even now he is one of the most underestimated men in the world, and perhaps that helps him. The people who consider themselves intellectuals or academics or experts generally had a preconceived attitude toward him of either contempt or amusement, along with the feeling that a person with his background as a movie actor couldn't be anything else. The honest ones among them were willing to admit that they had been wrong, and certainly a number of foreign leaders who initially knew of him only through that reputation changed their opinions of him very quickly. I stand by what I said in my book, *Fighting for Peace*.

QUESTION: In the book, you speak of the quality of the President's smile and the impact it had on the political atmosphere. Was that smile something that disappeared when he became angry?

MR. WEINBERGER: Yes, he has a good Irish temper. He can get pretty mad. He doesn't stay mad very long, but he is subject to a range of emotions.

QUESTION: Bryce Harlow, White House assistant serving under presidents Eisenhower and Nixon, once said that when President Eisenhower was angry, it was like looking down into a Bessemer furnace, but then it would disappear. Was Reagan that intense?

MR. WEINBERGER: No, I don't think so. President Reagan could get very angry and his eyes would become colder. These periods of anger did not last very long, but it was always quite apparent to anyone who knew him when he was not happy.

QUESTION: Was there any time during the administration, for instance after the assassination attempt or either of the surgeries, when he changed?

MR. WEINBERGER: No, he really hasn't changed to this day. He is a man who enjoys life, who likes people and wants them to be comfortable and happy. He is completely at peace with himself and he enjoys what he's doing. I never saw any change.

COMMENT: You weren't very happy about the appointment of Robert McFarlane as national security adviser, I gather.

MR. WEINBERGER: It wasn't the appointment; it was the way he handled the job after he was appointed. I didn't think he in any sense, had either the capability to do it or the willingness to acknowledge his lack of capability.

QUESTION: People have said in their balance sheets of President Reagan's strengths and weaknesses that he had a bit of difficulty in disciplining people and even more difficulty in firing them. Did he have any weakness in that area that you would want to mention?

MR. WEINBERGER: I don't know. A part of this view arose from the fact that the President is a very decent, nice human being with a great deal of compassion and consideration. He fully understands all the effects that firing somebody has on that person, so he would be hesitant to go that far. He tried to be careful with his basic appointments so that this kind of thing wouldn't arise. Because he is very considerate of people and a very compassionate person, he would certainly not take any pleasure in firing somebody or in exercising his temper or authority over them. If it was necessary, however, he would do so one way or another.

QUESTION: One thing the intellectuals have gotten after, of course, was the matter of what President Reagan read and how he responded to factual material. You have said that he read voluminously, knew what he wanted to accomplish, was easy to brief, and had a phenomenal memory. Could you say a little bit more about what he read?

MR. WEINBERGER: I think he read a great deal of general political and economic articles and periodicals. I don't know of any other general reading that he did, but he frequently came in primed with quotations from articles or points of view that he had heard or read about in the press. He would quote articles by a number of conservative economists and neoconservative writers, and it was apparent he had done a good bit of reading. He also took large amounts of reading matter home with him—government papers and things of that kind.

QUESTION: Did he ever ask you for something in the Churchill literature to look at?

MR. WEINBERGER: No, I don't know that he did. He talked about it a good bit, but of course he had people who worked on speeches for him and who would develop particular points that he was interested in.

QUESTION: What about his writing? Did he write some of his own speeches?

MR. WEINBERGER: He wrote many of his own speeches. His best speeches in many ways were those that he had written himself. He would write them out, usually by hand, and occasionally would use typewritten notes on the famous cards, but usually a great many of those cards were handwritten. Often he would edit in his own handwriting what had been written by others. He treated that material very carefully and put a lot of time in to it; that was important to him, and he did it very well.

QUESTION: Do you think he put great stock, from a leadership standpoint, in his press conferences and speeches?

MR. WEINBERGER: Yes, he handled them very well and prepared for them very carefully. I don't know how much stock he placed in them or how much he enjoyed doing them, but I think he regarded it as an obligation of his office to prepare carefully for them, and usually he was extremely effective in those duties.

QUESTION: Did he rehearse for and do retakes of speeches and press conferences?

MR. WEINBERGER: I don't think he rehearsed, but he was briefed before press conferences, particularly in Sacramento when he was governor, and again with somewhat larger groups while he was President.

QUESTION: Did his experience in Sacramento help him as a leader?

MR. WEINBERGER: Yes, without any question. That governorship was a major management and governmental task: California is the largest state in the Union and, I think, one of the seven or eight largest governmental entities in the world. In matters of budget and other problems, what they had out there was always a bit ahead of the kinds of problems that existed in other parts of the United States. It was an extraordinarily important learning experience for him.

QUESTION: Did things that happened in Sacramento, such as the tax increase, worry him, and did he talk about them?

MR. WEINBERGER: Yes, he paid close attention to everything that was happening, and he would only come to a decision such as that one reluctantly. In that case, as soon as we had straightened out the basic finances of the state, he wanted to give it back right away.

QUESTION: Is there anything on the other side of the ledger? Are there any weaknesses you feel are worthy of mention?

MR. WEINBERGER: I don't know. I'm sure there are. I've always hesitated to go into any of those. President Reagan violated the conventional wisdom so much that the press was always anxious to show that those violations were wrong and that he should do what everybody else did when they were in Washington. Any slight slip or forgetfulness or factual error would be picked up as some kind of major international story. Consequently, I never felt that I wanted to contribute any material to that side of the ledger. I think he did his job extremely well and that he was grossly underrated. He was a splendid governor and president, and the kind of person whom we needed as president, particularly at that time.

QUESTION: If it's true that he dealt more with the forest than he did with the trees, is there anything significant about the fact that a few of you who did try to master the last detail also had very good relationships with him?

MR. WEINBERGER: He did what the person in charge, the leader, should do. The contrast to that was President Carter allocating the time on the White House tennis courts. President Reagan wouldn't get into things like that. He was much more concerned with the broad policy.

For example, he wanted defense strengthened, and we went over with him the different kinds of weapon systems that would be needed, the strengthening of strategic forces, and he was very interested in whether or not there would be duplication or whether or not it would give us the kind of capabilities we would need if a crisis situation arose. He was obviously interested in the cost, but he set broad goals. He appointed people in whom he had confidence, and he worked with them carefully. If his goals weren't being achieved and people weren't coming through for him, then he would acknowledge that and try to change.

QUESTION: Every president talks about cabinet government but usually does not follow through on it. How did you feel about Reagan's organization for policy-making?

MR. WEINBERGER: In Sacramento, he worked with a small group of about five or six people who were department heads. They were in his immediate office, and it worked very well. We tried to set up a similar situation in Washington, but a number of people who were more favorable to the basic idea of presidential staff versus the Cabinet were able, in one way or another, to make sure that the more traditional form was established—that is, that the president would have his own staff, and the Cabinet would more or less run the departments. In Washington he didn't have close relationships with the heads of the various departments in the way that he did in Sacramento.

The important thing is that Reagan relied on people in whom he had confidence, and he worked with them. He always was accessible. I don't know about the other Cabinet members (I'm sure they did), but whenever I needed him I was able to talk with him. The basic difference between Sacramento and Washington was that in Sacramento he had had a great deal more contact with people and had utilized those who were heads of the major departments as his immediate staff, as opposed to having a separate immediate staff as he did in Washington.

QUESTION: I ask the next question with a little bit of hesitation, but it has come up in a couple of the oral histories we've had with others. Did the Californians have more access than others? One phrase that was used in one of our discussions was that "the California mafia threw a cocoon around him" for the first six months, and it was hard for some of the other people to know what he thought.

MR. WEINBERGER: I don't know. The access I had with the President didn't change in any of the seven years I was with him in Washington. It was always full and complete. I don't know anything about a "California mafia." The idea was that the people with whom he had worked closely were those to whom he would most naturally turn at first and rely on most heavily. Some of them were Californians, and some of them were not. James Baker, for example, was not a Californian, while Ed Meese and Michael Deaver had been with him in California and continued on. It is almost inevitable, however, that the White House staff and the people in the White House offices will want to ensure that other people's access to the president is through them, and that happens from time to time. Basically, though, the President saw the people he wanted to, and people who wanted to see him, as far as I know, were able to do so.

The people on whom he relied most were those he knew the best. Some were from California and some were not. Bill Casey, for example, was not a Californian; he was a New Yorker. Baker is from Texas. There were people whom he had come to know and had worked with on the campaign and otherwise, and, inevitably and naturally, those people were closest to him.

QUESTION: There have been a couple of journalistic statements to the effect that you felt frozen out at times. For example, did you ever feel that way regarding the SDI speech?

MR. WEINBERGER: No. There was one account published that said everybody else was frozen out and that only two people worked with the President on that matter. I did not feel frozen out. I knew of his great interest in it and that he was going to support it, although I didn't know of the precise timing of the speech until a week before. Of course, it was important that I know about it because of its impact on Europe. As I mentioned in my book, if I hadn't, it would have been very unfortunate to have gone to a NATO meeting and discussed various issues and then have the President, on the night the meeting ended, make an announcement of that kind. Thus, it was fortunate that I had friends who conveyed basic information to me about it. Still, the only issue was the timing of the speech. President Reagan's interest in SDI was not a surprise.

QUESTION: Would you comment on the idea mentioned by George Shultz and others, which I think goes back to Nixon, of a kind of "super cabinet?"

MR. WEINBERGER: That is essentially what we had in Sacramento. It was suggested that we try to do somewhat the same thing when Reagan took office in Washington. Basically, the opposition to that proposal went back to the idea that you couldn't get people to serve in the Cabinet if their positions were to be subordinated to a group-vice president type of organization in which groups of Cabinet departments were placed under an official who had more access to the President, which is essentially what we did in Sacramento. The idea is a good one, and I think it could work very well. Basically, in terms of time and coordinated policy, you try not to have too many people reporting to the chief executive, not because you want to keep the throne room to yourself or anything of that kind, but so that the president's span of control will be exercised through a reasonable number of people reporting directly to him.

QUESTION: So you think that the organization of the government for policy-making (especially the Cabinet) was fundamentally satisfactory? What about the White House and your relationship with it?

MR. WEINBERGER: I didn't have any problems. Whenever I wanted to see the President, I could. There were various people who had different ideas about the budget—people who thought we were spending too much on defense and people who worried that Reagan's presidency might be undermined if he appeared too hawkish. The President, however, never wavered or had any doubts, and he supported almost all of the recommendations I made. We were able to regain great military strength as a result. Still, there were a lot of people who felt that this was not a traditional approach—an approach in which you were supposed to compromise everything and end up with half or a quarter of what you had requested and which delays the process and costs much more in the long run. He never bought those temporizing, compromising sorts of arguments on issues on which he felt very strongly.

COMMENT: You did have trouble with David Stockman, I gather.

MR. WEINBERGER: I don't think Stockman was ever in any way committed to the President or to the President's goals or philosophy. I think Stockman did what a few people do: They accept a position and become part of the administration, and at the same time talk freely to others to demonstrate for conventional wisdom that they are really part of the administration, that they understand how difficult it is, and that the President doesn't really know what he's doing, but fortunately they're there. I think Stockman did a great deal of that, as probably a few others did as well. He tried to establish credentials on all sides of the fence, but he got caught when that interview with him was published.

The President is an extraordinarily kind and understanding person, but I don't think Stockman ever had his confidence after that. I don't think Stockman was ever committed in any way to what the President was trying to do. He decided at the beginning that he had to have a tax increase, and that in one way or another he was going to try to get it. He went behind the President's back many times. He would go to the Hill and talk with various congressmen and senators about how unwise it was for the President to have submitted the kind of defense budget he did. I suppose he did it with other departments too, but the defense budget was the one I knew about. This behavior was not that unusual. There will always be people with different ideas who believe the president isn't competent and thus feel that they have to manipulate the policy agenda.

COMMENT: You saw the same thing with Nixon.

MR. WEINBERGER: Oh, yes.

QUESTION: People often talk about competition on foreign and national security policy between the secretaries of state and defense and the National Security Council (NSC). How would you react to this statement? "Secretary of Defense Weinberger and Secretary of State Shultz engaged in continuing bureaucratic warfare that set the tone of nearly all debates. Determined to protect the corporate well-being of the Defense Department, Weinberger was fixed on avoiding a military involvement."

MR. WEINBERGER: I think that, inevitably, there are going to be differences of viewpoint between the State Department and Defense Department—institutional differences—and obviously some of the differences will reflect the differences in approach or philosophy of the people in office. For my part, I not only understood, but fully agreed with, strongly supported, and tried to implement as much as I could, the President's desire to strengthen our defenses. I believed that this objective was absolutely vital. For the most part, the State Department under George Shultz supported the increases in the defense budget. That was not a matter of dispute. However, on the other agendas the State Department inevitably had—signing treaties and agreements—I thought it was better to be concerned with what was in the agreement, not just the idea of getting an agreement.

With respect to the use of U.S. troops, I thought it was essential that we use the criteria I set out in that little talk to the Press Club. I believed it was essential that we have that in mind and not do what we had done in Vietnam and what a lot of people wanted us to do—committing a battalion here, and then a division, and then a couple of regiments, and so forth, never with the intention of winning, but always with the idea that the mere presence of American troops could make a difference, regardless of whether it was essential and whether or not other expedients had failed. That viewpoint probably stemmed from the fact that I had, and felt very keenly, the responsibility for the safety and the welfare of the troops. I also felt very strongly that we should use our military in proper situations; there would be plenty of sacrifices called for and everyone was prepared to make them, but we weren't prepared to rush in the American forces whenever anyone wanted them or whenever anyone thought that a token force or a little group here or there was going to make a difference. Given that responsibility, I was perhaps more cautious in the use of the troops than others who didn't have that responsibility.

QUESTION: Did the President ever discuss the National Press Club speech with you? Did he seem to agree with it?

MR. WEINBERGER: Yes, he did. He specifically agreed, and I had used parts of it before in ceremonies out at Arlington cemetery: the ideas that we should never enter a war that we didn't intend to win, that we should never enter a war unless it was important enough that we had to win it, and that we should never become involved in a war in which we did not intend to support the troops or were not willing to do everything possible.

That is why I've been so pleased with our actions in Panama and our actions right now in the Persian Gulf, because they seem to me to reflect that philosophy completely—that you go in with all the strength you need, but you only go in when it's absolutely essential to do so. The idea of going in to contain something, going in and not allowing the military to fight beyond a certain parallel, going in because some other government wants us to but when it is not absolutely vital to our own interest, or when all the diplomatic resources have not been exhausted are things that I opposed very strongly. I do not believe that the President ever disagreed with any of that, but there are a lot of people who are petulant about not being able to persuade him that we should bomb somebody occasionally or to take some military action that had a good adventurous ring to it. Those courses of action would do nothing but drag us in to areas that we didn't have to get in to and would be a major risk to the troops.

QUESTION: What were your views on arms control?

MR. WEINBERGER: I believe arms control agreements have been violated a great deal in the past. I felt that there was an enormous amount of desire for the political benefits of signing an agreement without nearly enough consideration as to what was in it, and I frankly didn't trust the Soviets on the basis of their previous record of breaking treaties. I thought there were arms control agreements that were good, but that the process itself was not the goal—the idea was to get a good agreement. Frequently we would run into the argument: "Well, you've got to give way, to give the Soviets things they want, or they won't sign. If they won't sign you can't get an agreement, and if you don't have an agreement it would be a horrible blot on the presidency." I always point to the INF (Intermediate-range Nuclear Forces) agreement that took seven years of negotiations to complete. I supported it from the very beginning and recommended that we sign it. A lot of the others, however, were strongly against it. The State Department at that time was strongly against the zero option. However, by holding out and not giving in to all the Soviet demands, we eventually got exactly the agreement we wanted, which was, as a matter of fact, exactly the agreement that I had proposed and recommended and which the President supported in October 1981.

QUESTION: If the President had had another term, would he have gotten a strategic arms agreement?

MR. WEINBERGER: I think so, but again they would have had to be agreements that were in our national interest. It's much more difficult to verify agreements that don't call for a complete elimination of the weapon system. There was always tremendous pressure to have an agreement from the State Department and from many in the academic community, as well as from those who had worked in arms control. Arguments were always made that the process was a two-way street, that you had to give way in order to obtain an agreement. However, I never felt that the process was more important than the substance. I always wanted to know what was in an agreement and that if we couldn't get an agreement that was in our interest, it was better not to have any. That was a fundamental point of difference, but the President, I think, agreed with me fully.

QUESTION: Was Reykjavík as bad as Henry Kissinger says it was?

MR. WEINBERGER: Reykjavík had a lot of the elements of a very unstructured poker game in which Gorbachev seemed to be trying to get the maximum amount of favorable world publicity. He was offering things that I'm sure he was not prepared either to accept or to adhere to, even if an agreement had been reached. The tone was "I'll cut 25 percent." "Well, I'll cut 50 percent and I'll see you"—things like that. I thought that was a format that wasn't right for that kind of meeting. We were supposed to have the next summit meeting in the United States, and summits, everyone had previously agreed, were supposed to be carefully prepared, with predictable results. Again, however, there was great passion for a meeting, and the President was very anxious to improve relationships with the Soviets and had great confidence in his ability to negotiate with all different kinds of people, so he agreed to their proposal for a quick meeting in Iceland. He was pushed very hard by a number of people who thought the only way to improve relationships was to have meetings.

I think the meeting at Reykjavík was premature. It was in the wrong place and at the wrong time, and a great deal might have happened if it hadn't been for the fact that the President recognized the dangers, pulled back, and refused to give up SDI. That infuriated a great many people who were against SDI from the beginning, because it violated the conventional wisdom that you're not supposed to have any defenses. In every way, it was the wrong meeting at the wrong place and time. It was saved because the President was very firm; even though he recognized all the political advantages of shaking hands and signing things, he decided that there were other things that were more important. That was the point I had been urging all along, so it didn't matter whether I was physically present or not—the result was important. I think all was in peril for a time, but the President saved it in the end.

NARRATOR: Mr. Secretary, thank you.

II

PERSONALITY
AND POLICY-MAKING

CHAPTER 4

REAGAN AS DECISIONMAKER*

JOHN C. WHITEHEAD

NARRATOR: It may be superfluous to qualify the witness as we sometimes do in our Reagan Oral history series. Certainly all of you know that John C. Whitehead was deputy secretary of state, and many times acting secretary during Secretary Shultz's absences between 1985 and January 1989. He was born in Evanston, Illinois, raised in Montclair, New Jersey. He received his bachelor's degree from Haverford College and his MBA from Harvard University. He also has honorary degrees from a number of institutions, including Pace University, Rutgers, Haverford, and probably others by now. Mr. Whitehead has a distinguished wartime career as well, having served on the *USS Thomas Jefferson* and participated in three landings—Normandy, Iwo Jima, and Okinawa.

In his business and banking career, he worked for Goldman, Sachs & Company starting as a junior statistician and rising to senior partner and co-chairman. He also served as director of the American District Telegraph Company, Crompton and Knowles Corporation, Dillard Department Stores, Household International, the Pillsbury Company, and others. Additionally, he has served as director of the New York Stock Exchange and as director and chairman of the Securities Industry Association.

Finally, since leaving government Mr. Whitehead has been president of the Harvard Board of Overseers, a member of the Board of Rockefeller University, and chairman of the United

---

Presented in a Forum at the Miller Center on 18 May 1991.

Nations Association of the United States, the Andrew W. Mellon Foundation, The Asia Society, and International House. He has also served as a member of the board of the Carnegie Corporation, Outward Bound, and a number of other organizations. We are thrilled that John Whitehead could join us and we are looking forward to our discussion.

MR. WHITEHEAD: Thank you very much.   Since people are always interested in how I came to be deputy secretary of state, I will tell you that story, because I think President Reagan's efforts to attract me show some of his character traits. As has been said, I worked for 37 years as an investment banker on Wall Street, and although I retired from Goldman, Sachs after serving as chairman for 10 years, I continued to make my office there.

Late one afternoon I was sitting in my office when the phone rang. It was George Shultz who, as you may know, is rather cryptic in his style and not a talkative fellow. He said, "Can you be in my office at 8 o'clock tomorrow morning?" It was then 6:00 p.m., and it quickly flashed through my mind that there was no way that I could take the first shuttle in the morning down to Washington and be in his office at 8:00 a.m. I would have to go down that night, and that would mean that I would not be able to go home for dinner. I thought of all these things, but I said, "Yes, of course." His response was, "Good, I'll see you then," and I could tell he was about to hang up. I quickly said, "George, if you could tell me what this is about, I would be better able to advise or consult with you." He responded by saying that it was not something he could talk about on the phone, and after a pause, I said, "All right, I'll see you at 8 o'clock."

I thought to myself, what could the secretary of state, whom I knew slightly but not very well, want to talk about with a recently retired investment banker? It occurred to me that either Argentina or Brazil must be about to go bankrupt, and that because he had never been in office when a country went bankrupt, he wanted to know from an old investment banker with a lot of international financial experience what he ought to be worried about.

I called the library of Goldman, Sachs and asked for information on the current economic conditions of Argentina and Brazil. Fifteen minutes later, two big files came up, one on Brazil and one on Argentina. I took a taxi to the airport, got myself a hotel reservation, checked into the hotel, and studied the material in those two files.

I arrived in Shultz's office at the appointed hour carrying the two folders, and the first thing he said was, "It's nice to have you here. I'm glad you could come on such short notice. We are going to see the President." "Well," I thought to myself, "it must be *both* Argentina and Brazil!" We got into Shultz's limousine and drove to the White House. In five minutes, the three of us were in the Oval Office. Not even Don Regan was there!

The President said, "The purpose of all this is to invite you, to urge you, to accept an appointment as deputy secretary of state," which was the number two job in the State Department. I gulped. I had the two manila folders with me, one under each arm, so I shifted them to one side and laid them on the floor. I didn't have any experience in diplomacy or international affairs, so I didn't really feel qualified for the job. After saying how complimented I was to be asked, I said, "Mr. President, if you had asked me to do something in the Treasury Department, the World Bank, or the Federal Reserve Board, I know how to run a bank or financial institution, but I don't know anything about international relations." "Well," said the President with that little smile of his, "there aren't any openings there." That took the steam out of me a bit. Even though I didn't feel qualified, I said I would think about it; they kept telling me why they thought I could do the job.

I told them that I was due to leave that night for a long-planned trip to Hong Kong and Tokyo, but that upon my return in ten days I would have an answer for them. I was about ready to get up, but a silence ensued. Finally, the President said, "Ten days is an awful long time, and we really need to fill this job. Why don't we compromise. Why don't you go to Hong Kong, where you plan to spend three days, and then come right back and scratch the Tokyo trip?" There was another silence before I said that I would do that. The President then said, "You're going to be there three days. The fourth day is next Friday. I'll see you here at 3:15 p.m. next Friday, OK?" I said, "Fine."

I went to Hong Kong, spent my three days, and returned, all the time thinking about whether I should take the job. At the appointed hour, I went first to Shultz's office and then we went through the same routine: We got in the car with the Secret Service, drove through the White House gate, and arrived in the

Oval Office. Once again, there were the three of us. The President looked at his watch and said, "It's 3:15 p.m. You've been to Hong Kong; you are right on time. I have you down for a 15-minute appointment, but I told my secretary that if we are not out at 3:30 p.m., she should cancel my 3:30 appointment so that we can keep talking. As a matter of fact, I have told her that she should continue to cancel my appointments for the rest of the afternoon, through the dinner hour and right up until 10:30 p.m. At 10:30 p.m., I have to go to bed." He added that they now had seven hours to persuade me to take this job, and he asked where I would like to begin.

On the way from Shultz's office to the White House, I had told Shultz that I had decided to accept the job. Neither of us had been able to tell the President yet, so I said, "Mr. President, as I told George on the way over, I've decided to accept if you still want me. Despite my lack of qualifications for the job, I'll be glad to do it, and I will give it my best." His response was, "That's wonderful. We're glad to have you on the team. You will find it a wonderful experience." Then he looked at his watch, and said, "Well, we have 12 more minutes. Let's go for a walk in the garden." He opened the French doors in the Oval Office, put his arm around my shoulder—it was a wonderful spring day in April—and we walked around the Rose Garden for 12 minutes.

During that time he told me how he too, upon retiring from his commercial activities, had been urged by friends in California to get involved in politics and run for governor, and how he had been reluctant to do it, envisioning a different kind of retirement. He said that he was delighted that I, at about the same age he had been when he entered government, had decided to do the same thing. He added that he had never regretted it and knew that I wouldn't either.

If I had not been a fan of the President prior to that, I certainly became one with the arm-around-the-shoulder thing and the 12-minute walk in the Rose Garden. This story reveals a couple of things about the President. He was very tough in that negotiation! He twisted my arm very hard in suggesting that I cancel my trip to Tokyo, where a speech I was to deliver had already been scheduled and invitations had gone out. It was awkward for me to cancel, but he didn't hesitate to twist my arm very hard. I wondered when I heard the business about having seven hours to persuade me to take the job what would have happened if I had decided not to take it. I probably would have ended up changing my mind.

Although the President always had a genial, friendly, smiling manner, he also had an underlying toughness that came through every once in a while. Sometimes you didn't even notice how tough he had been, because he had been so nice. He would sometimes make a decision you didn't agree with, but you could sense his inner strength that was not always visible.

I started in my new job, and because of my lack of knowledge, I did a lot of learning. There were many briefings from the wonderful State Department Foreign Service people, who were eager to have somebody on board who respected them, listened to them, and took advice from them. I didn't always follow their advice, but I always listened to it.

Two of my children presented me right off with two sets of flash cards. From one set I learned the capitals of 150 countries. A typical card had "Great Britain" on one side and "London" on the other. The other set of cards had heads of states listed; for example, "Great Britain" on one side, and "Mrs. Thatcher" on the other. All of this was to prepare me for my hearing before the Senate Foreign Relations Committee, which political appointees must go through before they take on their full responsibilities.

As an aside, I am reminded of a story following the announcement of my appointment that appeared on the Saturday after the second meeting in the White House. It was a slow news day, so the story and my picture appeared on the front page of the *New York Times*. I lived then in the little town of Essex Fells, New Jersey, where I had lived most of my life and where the only commercial establishment is a filling station run by a man named Ed Peeler, who is a lifelong friend. I have always had my car serviced at his filling station.

On that Saturday morning, I drove in as I usually did to fill the car with gas and chat with Ed. He came out to the car, put the hose in the tank, and stopped at my car window to talk to me. He said, "I see you're moving to Washington." I answered, "Yep." He then asked if I was going to work for the government, and again I answered, "Yep." Ed responded: "Too bad; if Goldman, Sachs had had a better pension plan, you wouldn't have had to." That is the story I often remembered during those dark moments in office. I remembered Ed Peeler's reaction, and I sometimes thought that he was right.

The next time I saw the President was the day after I was confirmed by the Senate and sworn into office. Shultz left on a long trip to Asia, and for three weeks I was to be the acting secretary. The President called me in and said he had a terrible problem that he didn't know if I could help him with or not. It concerned the "Big Seven" meeting in Washington that the President was hosting this time, and he noted that the heads of the other six members of the Big Seven were all coming as his guests to spend a week together. The President said that the agendas for the meeting were being developed, but that President Bettino Craxi of Italy had just said he wasn't going to come. It would be pretty insulting and embarrassing if he didn't come. The reason Craxi was upset was due to the *Achille Lauro* incident, in which some terrorists had boarded the cruise ship while it was in Italy with 400 Americans aboard and an elderly American in a wheelchair was killed. The terrorist who planned that activity, a man named Abu Abbas, was arrested by the Italian government. However, because there was no information permitting them to hold him, he was released. He escaped from Italy and disappeared back into the terrorist world. President Reagan was horrified by this announcement and criticized the Italian government quite sharply for having failed to bring Abu Abbas to justice.

Craxi saw the incident quite differently. He believed that his efforts and the efforts of his police had saved 399 Americans on that ship from a terrible terrorist tragedy; he was so delighted that only one person had been killed in the incident that he thought he deserved to be complimented, rather than criticized. The President asked me if I could do anything about this problem, and suggested that I go over and see him, which I did. Craxi was very reluctant to see me, and in order to do so under these tense circumstances, I had to tell him that I was the direct representative of the President who would have come himself if he had been able to. We eventually met. The meeting was very stiff and formal with no opening pleasantries at all. Craxi and Giulio Andreotti, who was then the foreign minister and more recently had become the prime minister, were on one side of the table and Max Rabb, our ambassador to Italy for eight years, a feisty, talkative little lawyer from New York, and I were on the other side.

I kept mentioning President Reagan so Craxi wouldn't feel awkward speaking to a lowly deputy secretary of state. Craxi had a yellow pad in front of him filled with notes of all the many things he wanted to get off his chest. I said to Craxi that the President had asked me to try and clear up the misunderstanding, that I knew that his government's views on the *Achille Lauro* incident differed from ours, and that I very much wanted to hear their views in order to carry them back to the President. Well, that is what he had been waiting for, and he started talking. One by one he turned over the yellow pages on which he had prepared detailed notes about his side of the story. Every once in a while Max Rabb heard him say something that was not accurate or a little strong. Knowing that it would have been a mistake to interrupt, each time I saw Max begin to rise up out of his chair to make an objection, I would squeeze his knee under the table. (He tells me that that knee is still sore.) One hour and 15 minutes later Craxi finally came to the end of his notes. Then it was as if the air had been let out of a balloon. Craxi had finished telling us what he had wanted to say, and we had listened to him.

After that, Craxi couldn't have been nicer. I told him we now had his views on the incident, many of which we were not aware of, and that he had helped us to better understand his point of view. I said that I hoped he would visit the President the following week at the Big Seven meeting, to which he replied that he would be delighted to come. I cabled the President back from Rome that night saying that Craxi would attend the meeting. That was my first mission, so I was off to a good start.

I have many memories of the President, but I will mention just two other interesting incidents. Most of my visits with the President occurred when George Shultz was out of Washington while I was acting secretary. It was then that I would go to Cabinet and National Security Council meetings, so most of my contact with the President was when George was away.

Remember the day we took military action against Gadhafi by bombing terrorist bases in Libya in what was called a "surgical strike"? There is no such thing as surgical strike, but there was a bombing attack that was very controversial. We justified it on the grounds that while military action is generally not an appropriate response, terrorists were being trained in Libya, and the country did serve as a base for some wicked international terrorist groups. So we took military action, hoping to intimidate Gadhafi into discontinuing his support for terrorism, and indeed it did. We have heard very little about Gadhafi or from Gadhafi since that attack.

In any event, the final meeting to discuss whether or not to go forward with military action took place on a Sunday night in the White House. I was spending the weekend in Williamsburg when I received a call to hurry back to Washington for an 8 o'clock evening meeting at the White House. Those who believe that President Reagan was not always the final decisionmaker should have been at that meeting. They would have seen, as I often did, that no one but President Reagan himself made the big decisions. He listened to others, but ultimately decided for himself.

The meeting lasted about two and a half hours and was over at 10:30 p.m., the President's bedtime. It began with a presentation from the military regarding the details of the action contemplated, an evaluation of the casualties that could be expected, and the kind of results that might be achieved. Eight congressional leaders were present at the meeting, four from the Senate and four from the House. They were the top leaders of both organizations, because this was a consultation with Congress prior to a military decision.

After the one-hour presentation from the secretary of defense and the chairman of the Joint Chiefs of Staff, the meeting entered into a general discussion during which the President went around the room and called first on those of us who were from the administration and then on each member of Congress to give our views on the issue. My assignment was to give the State Department's view of the diplomatic aspects of the event—how we thought our allies and other Arab countries would react to our action and how we should go about informing these countries of our action—and the rationale for it. Then the discussion opened up to include the congressmen.

There was quite a lot of criticism—reservation would be a better word—expressed about the action. So the President went around a second time and said, "Some of you have expressed your reservations, and my people have tried to respond to them, but now we need to decide whether or not to go forward. It is not too late to call this off; I would not have called you in here for a perfunctory meeting. I'm really listening to what you have to say."

He went around the room a second time, and not one member of Congress recommended that he call off the operation. They still had reservations, of course; we all did. There are pros and cons with any tough decision. They also made it clear that it was the President's decision, and that they were only being consulted and advised. So it went forward, and in retrospect, I think it was a success and achieved its objectives.

I saw the President in the process of making a final decision at that meeting. He said, "My decision is that we will go forward with this attack as recommended by my secretary of defense and by the chairman of the Joint Chiefs of Staff." We all knew when we left that meeting that the military action would go forward, and it did. The attack took place the next morning. The President made a very tough and controversial decision, and he made it in a deliberate way.

The other incident that I would like to describe occurred somewhat later. The State Department, at least in the beginning, was sort of out of the loop and was not well informed by the National Security Council and the White House staff as to what was taking place during the Iran-contra affair. Rumors had begun to circulate, not so much about the diversion of funds to the contras, but more about how the White House had agreed to sell arms to Iran when it was against our policy to do so, thereby prompting the Senate Foreign Relations Committee to hold hearings on this question.

The first witness was to be the secretary of state, but unfortunately he was going to be out of the country at the time of the hearing on a long-planned and very legitimate trip. The person principally responsible for our general policy in Iran was the number three man in the State Department, Under Secretary for Political Affairs Mike Armacost. He had been designated to testify regarding our policy toward Iran, including our efforts to search out moderate leaders in Iran with whom we could have a reasonable dialogue and who might come into leadership positions in the future. His testimony was to deal with how we were going about that effort.

Shultz, Armacost, and I had a meeting the morning the testimony was to be given, as we usually did to match notes on what each of us was going to do during the day. Armacost, at that meeting, said that because he was a career foreign service officer, and the issue was developing as a political one, he wondered if it might be more appropriate for a political appointee rather than a foreign service office to give the testimony. Suddenly I saw them both looking at me, and being a good soldier, though still a somewhat naive soldier, I was designated to give the testimony. I had only a couple of hours to prepare for it. I read over the testimony that had been prepared for Armacost to give and asked questions about it.

The hearings lasted for three hours. It was a long and grueling day, certainly the worst I had in my job at the State Department. It was also a big media show with revelations about certain bad incidents, disorganization, and a lack of communication within the administration. In my testimony, I tried to defend the policies of the administration and the President and give our rationale for wanting contact with Iran. I also denied any knowledge of arms sales.

I was steadfast in my defense of the President, but I didn't give a very good answer to a question posed by one congressman from my home state of New Jersey regarding the President's announcement that during our efforts to find moderate leaders in Iran there had been a substantial reduction in terrorist activities emanating from Iran. Instead of saying that the President was poorly advised or badly informed, I said, "Well, I hate to disagree with my President, but . . ." I went on to explain that there had been absolutely no reduction in terrorist activity. In fact, there had been an increase in terrorist activity.

When I went back to my office, I turned on my television and I was all over the tube. None of the nice things I had said were mentioned, but the comment—"I hate to disagree with my President but . . ."—was on the 7 o'clock evening news, and I thought, oh boy, am I ever in trouble! What I had intended, and what was evident for anybody who saw my entire transcript, was a sterling albeit somewhat difficult defense of the administration. As seen on television, however, it appeared to be an attack on the White House by the deputy secretary of state.

I immediately wrote the President a handwritten note, which he received that night, saying that I hoped he hadn't thought I was being disloyal. I said that the thrust of my testimony was positive, but I was afraid it was being misinterpreted by the press.

Early the next morning, President Reagan called me over, and I thought, "Well, it's been a nice year in Washington. Here I go back to Wall Street." The President, however, thanked me for the note, and said, "You're doing a terrific job and I have no thought of making a change. You have been loyal, supportive, intelligent, and imaginative." He also said, "Everybody has these bad moments, and I certainly have had my share. This will pass, and I just want you to know that I support everything you have done."

Then he got that little twinkle in his eye and said, "But, let me tell you what happened yesterday when I heard about this." He said that he had had a very full schedule and had gotten back to his desk at about 6:00 p.m., where he worked until just before 7:00 p.m., signing papers. Then, he had gone upstairs to the family quarters, taken off his jacket, tie, and shoes, put on his slippers, and poured himself a drink before settling down in front of the television to watch the evening news. He then said to me, "Do you know, John, how when you turn on the television set, the sound comes on first but the picture doesn't come on for a few seconds while the tube warms up?" I said yes. "Well," he said, "I turned on the set and the sound came on, and I heard somebody say, 'I hate to disagree with my president.' John, I said to myself, now who the hell is that? Then the picture came on, and John, it was you!" He said, "I couldn't believe it." It was that wonderful human trait that he had. He made me feel good, but then made me realize that this incident had presented a problem for him too. I had not done a very smart or intelligent thing, and I should have been less careless after three hours of grueling testimony.

QUESTION: Would you tell us about the time you went over and met Saddam Hussein—the circumstances surrounding the meeting and your thoughts at the time.

MR. WHITEHEAD: I did see Saddam Hussein when I was on a tour of the Middle East sometime after the meeting that I described with Craxi, and I have to confess that I was favorably impressed with him. The cable I sent after my visit with him reflects that I was favorably impressed.

I had read a lot about him before the visit, so I was aware of his history; I knew it was not all wonderful, nor did I find any saint. Hussein was dressed in a business suit, not in a general's uniform. He greeted me on time in his office, as expected, and I would say that the conversation was very businesslike. He was intelligent and understanding.

The subject of our conversation was terrorism, as the United States was trying to put down terrorism and prevent Iraq from serving as a haven for terrorists. Hussein made strong statements about how Iraq found world terrorism reprehensible, and there was no evidence at that time that Iraq had been a haven for terrorists or had served as a terrorist base in any way. We were afraid, however, that it might become one, so the thrust of my remarks was to warn him that the United States would find it very reprehensible if we should find that he was protecting terrorists in any way, such as issuing passports, or financing them, as some other Arab countries had.

Hussein could not have been more forthright in condemning terrorism, and he seemed like a rational and reasonable fellow. I compared him with other Arab leaders who are now our strong friends and allies but who seemed very much from another world. For example, in the United Arab Emirates and Saudi Arabia and Kuwait, the typical time for a meeting with a visiting dignitary is sometime around midnight. Well, that puts you off a bit, but an appointment is never scheduled for a specific time because that would be insulting to the king. When you arrive in the country, and this applies no matter what your rank, you check into your hotel and notify the palace that you are there. Then you wait to be summoned, sometimes for a long time. Once in a while, they are adaptable and summon you earlier, but the normal time is sometime after 10:30 at night when they appear to go to work.

Once you get to the palace, the customs seem strange and the dialogue is awkward. Sometimes you finish whatever remarks you came to make and get no response; there is a dead silence, which you don't know quite how to handle. You might then ask a question, and get another dead silence. Anyhow, it can be a very strange and awkward experience. In any event, that is my slightly embarrassing recollection of Saddam Hussein in comparison with other Arab leaders.

QUESTION: It's nice to have confirmation of the human side of President Reagan; I am sure we all appreciated it through the eight years that he was in the White House. Were you ever present when he was uptight or hung up on something? I have never heard anybody refer to a time when he was hung up. He was apparently always loose, and that doesn't seem quite human.

MR. WHITEHEAD: I don't think I ever saw him except when he was relaxed. He had a marvelous ability to step back from the fray and look at a situation in perspective. It's very easy when you are in Washington to get all caught up in some little thing that you are responsible for and think that it is the center of the world. Reagan never did that; he never allowed himself to get that way.

Another incident that comes to mind involves the tiny country of Suriname in South America, which used to be called Dutch Guiana. At one point toward the end of the administration, it looked as though there was about to be a revolution in Suriname and that the government might be overthrown by what we considered to be a much less stable and desirable element in Suriname. While Shultz was away and I was acting secretary, we received information that the coup might take place that weekend, and that the United States would have to respond to this coup if indeed it did take place. Would we recognize the new government or condemn it? Would we support the old government? Might we even send military troops to defend the popularly elected government that then existed?

I decided that this was a matter that I really needed to speak to the President about. It was urgent, as the coup was expected to take place that night or the next morning. So I made an appointment to go see the President and gave him all the information we had on Suriname.

"Suriname, " he said. "Would you show me where it is on the map?" I wasn't surprised that he didn't know where it was; a lot of people don't know where Suriname is. So I showed him where it was on the map, and he said, "You said it used to be Dutch Guiana. Do the Dutch have an interest in this, and what are they going to do about it?" I told him the Dutch did have an interest because there were still many Dutch-owned businesses and Dutch citizens there. The President also asked me how many Americans were in Suriname—I think the number was 300—and whether I thought that any of their lives would be in danger when the coup took place." When I told him that I didn't think so, he said, "Let's wait and see what happens; let's not make too big an incident of it." Of course he was right. I had thought at the time that maybe he wasn't as alarmed as he should have been, but he had stepped back from the incident and put it in perspective. Incidentally, the coup never took place. The Dutch didn't take any action, and we didn't take any action. For a moment Suriname was a small country where something big might have exploded. There are other countries in the region where a coup might have had an explosive effect, but it never happened. The President was right to downplay it.

QUESTION: To draw on the rest of your background, what do you see for the future of America, considering all the problems we now face, one of the major ones being the enormous deficit that really took off during the Reagan administration? What do you see as America's position in the world in the next five or ten years?

MR. WHITEHEAD: It's a good question, and one that all of us should think more about than we do, but I see our assets as far larger than our liabilities. The big change that has taken place in the world is the collapse of communism. Remember that since the end of World War II, the United States, standing for democracy and freedom, has been confronting countries standing for communist ideals in a battle that has generally led to a standoff. Thus, nothing much was accomplished in terms of the many problems the world faced during that 45-year period following World War II.

Now communism has collapsed. They have thrown in the towel and it becomes more evident every day that they are not going to return to the kind of dictatorship that existed previously in the Soviet Union and Eastern Europe. We know now what a complete and total failure it was, politically and economically; it did not bring a better life for its people.

I believe this leaves the United States in the world's leadership position, despite our many problems. People talk about Japan and Germany, but Japan's economy is only half of what ours is, and Germany's is less than half of ours. We still have by far the largest economy and the principles and moral leadership that permit us to lead the world. For the first time since World War II we have an opportunity to deal with some of the world problems like the environment and narcotics—world problems that no single country can solve within its own borders, but which must be solved on a global basis. So I see tremendous opportunity for the United States in the next ten years to lead the world forward to a better world. I also see problems such as the huge deficits that we have accumulated, though I do not think they are insurmountable.

QUESTION: Your answer to the last question suggests that you believe the United States can play a leadership role through the United Nations and other international organs. The Reagan administration, however, seems to have initially advocated a unilateral approach, scorning international cooperation and the United Nations on the whole. Will you tell us about the Reagan administration's turnaround on that issue?

MR. WHITEHEAD: I'm glad you asked that question; I am very proud of the administration's turnaround. During the administration's first term, Republicans, generally, were very anti-United Nations and anti-world cooperation. We saw the United Nations as an organization which was not working to our interests and which was dominated by the Soviets, or really, by a combination of Third World nations, each with one vote. The number of United Nations members had grown from less than 50 countries when it began to its present number of more than 150, incorporating all of the small countries given their independence after World War II. All of these countries had their own vote, but because the money for the United Nations was put up by the larger developed countries, particularly the United States, the smaller countries did not contribute much to the budget. They did, however, benefit from U.N. expenditures. The budget of the United Nations and participating agencies grew quickly without any influence or control from the United States or other developed countries. Thus, we found the United Nations to be constantly passing resolutions condemning the United States for many of its actions. Gradually with time, partly due to the collapse of communism and the vastly improved relationship between the United States and the Soviet Union, the President changed. George Shultz and I made an effort to convince him that the world situation had now changed, and the United Nations was now an organization that could work to our interest.

In the last two years of the Reagan administration, the President's budget included recommendations for full funding for the United Nations. Though Congress did not appropriate the money for full funding the first of those two years, it did pass full funding in the last year. The Bush administration has not only continued the policy since, but is even providing funds to pay up our back dues.

The United States leadership through world organizations is what the decade of the future holds. The United Nations is a big and important key to that strategy, and the United States must therefore remain actively and positively involved in that organization.

QUESTION: Will Gorbachev survive and where does Yeltsin fit into the picture?

MR. WHITEHEAD: That is a good question to which I don't really have an answer. I do point out to you, though, something that many people are surprised to realize. Two years ago, the Soviets adopted a new constitution with great pride. For them, it was an event much like the adoption of our Constitution over 200 years ago. The adoption of that constitution was a big event for all Soviet citizens. The new constitution provides for a president, and in their first free election Gorbachev was elected president for a five-year term by an overwhelming vote. Two years have passed since then.

I always say that I think Gorbachev will survive. The Soviet people are not going to vote out the constitution that I think they respect. They may not like Gorbachev, the slow progress toward a market economy, or the chaos in their economy. They may force him to share his power with others, but I doubt that he will actually depart unless he, himself, becomes so discouraged that he quits, as Shevardnadze did. However, he will probably be there for three more years, varying his policies so as to adapt to pressures from both the left and the right [Editor's note: But history moved too fast].

As for Yeltsin, I sat with him at dinner on his visit to the United States, and I was not very favorably impressed. He seemed to be a critic without any plans of his own, which is an easy populist position to put yourself in when you are out of office. You can criticize and complain but be free of any responsibility. Now that Yeltsin is in a position of responsibility, however, I do see much more responsible conduct and statements on his part. The current administration in Russia is his, and he has to defend what he is doing to his people; he is subject now to many more political questions. Still, I suspect that Yeltsin may be more of a passing figure than Gorbachev is, and that other leadership will emerge.

Though I don't think the Soviet Union will fall apart, I do think there will be a much looser confederation of provinces or republics in the Soviet Union with much more power delegated to the republics than was allowed under the Moscow-controlled regimes of the past. For the republics, including the Baltic states, to operate with complete independence with no economic or political relations whatsoever would be a very difficult thing to do. I suspect that all of the republics will continue to maintain some kind of affiliation within a loose federation. From the U.S. point of view, that is not a bad result, because a central dominant Soviet government is unlikely to occur again, or at least not for a very long period of time. The greater the decentralization of power that takes place and the greater the independence of the republics, the better it is for us and for the rest of the world.

QUESTION: Are you optimistic that Eastern Europe, the Soviet Union, and the Baltics will become democratic, more or less free enterprise states, without being toppled along the way by economic problems or a new kind of dictatorship?

MR. WHITEHEAD: Yes, I am optimistic that this will happen. Reform is moving forward more slowly than we would probably like in those countries, but at least it is moving. As long as that progress continues, we can be optimistic about all the countries in Eastern Europe.

Eastern Europe is a region for which I had a special responsibility. After I had been in my job for about a year, I looked around to see what part of the world in which I could take a special interest, and I selected Eastern Europe. I saw that the secretary himself would have to be the principal person dealing with the Soviet Union, but that he would not be able to pay the same attention to Eastern Europe. He couldn't visit the capitals of Eastern Europe with the same frequency that he visited Moscow.

So I obtained authority to take on Eastern Europe and began to travel there when it was an unpopular thing to do. Many right-wing people thought it was atrocious for a good American to visit Communist dictators like Todor Zhivkov, Nicolae Ceausescu, Wojciech Jaruzelski, and others. In fact, before my first trip the criticism was so strong from the ultra right wing, who were always quoting the President, that I decided I had better talk to the

President myself before I embarked on another fiasco (this was after my contra mistake).

I told the President that I had planned to make a trip to Eastern Europe because I didn't think we could find out what was going on in these countries or convey to them what we thought about their oppression unless we visited them. I told him that I was planning a trip, whom I was proposing to see, and what I was going to say to each of them. Then, I asked him if that sounded OK to him. He said he thought it sounded terrific, and that it was what I should be doing. I said, "But all of these people, including some on your staff, are telling me that you feel that these are all evil countries and that we shouldn't have anything to do with them." The President, however, said that we were trying to improve our relations with the Soviet Union, and it would be great if I could improve our relations with Eastern Europe as well. So even though the right wing continued to attack, I knew that their leader, who is not as far right wing as some people think, was with me.

Through this experience and a number of other similar ones, I learned that if I spoke with him myself, I found that on many subjects he wasn't the extremist that right-wing Republicans thought he was. He was a very human person, and when he had thought through the Eastern European issue, he realized that progress could be made. Indeed, a lot of progress was made with the Eastern European countries in terms of weaning them from their complete dependence on the Soviet Union. Our idea was a good one and it worked.

I had another similar experience with the President in regard to some environmental issues. Reagan was certainly never known as the environmental president, and some of my colleagues in the administration seemed to think that any attempt to improve the environment was wrong. I understood that we couldn't impose huge penalties on American businesses that polluted without risking their financial health. We needed a balanced policy encouraging or insisting that they decrease their pollution, but not to the point where it would put them out of business. Still, members of the administration thought that environmental efforts that in any way restrained the freedom of people to pollute at their will were wrong.

At one point, a world conference was under way negotiating reductions of hydrocarbons, with the State Department representing the United States. A small group of right-wingers, including a couple of Cabinet officers, had taken the position that the United States should not agree to any restraints on the pollutants causing the hole in the ozone layer. I went to the President and suggested that we had an opportunity to lead the world in controlling the particular pollutants causing the ozone problem. I told him that we could accomplish this before the end of his administration, except that this effort was being forestalled by those who were against it. I asked him if he was really against it, and he said that he was not. So we went ahead with our program and the flak died down at the President's instructions. Now we have a wonderful treaty that over a period of five years will control all pollutants detrimental to the ozone layer.

The treaty met with very little opposition from industry. Those businesses had simply not wanted it to go into effect suddenly, because it would badly hurt them and throw people out of jobs. They wanted a five-year break-in period, which was reasonable. Since, for example, materials necessary for refrigeration systems were involved, new nonpolluting chemicals had to be found to replace them. So, the five-year break-in period was sensible and balanced. In brief, that is how we achieved a good treaty, and the President deserves much credit for it because it involved his overruling his extremist allies.

NARRATOR: The third area that you specialized in concerned administrative reform in the State Department. As I remember, you came forward with a pretty tough report about some of the cutbacks that were needed, but later dealt with that issue with great moderation. What were the President's views regarding the State Department?

MR. WHITEHEAD: If you had posed the question in that manner, the President would have said that he found a lot of faults in the State Department. However, if you had asked him what he thought of the job George Shultz was doing, he would have said "terrific," or if you had asked about specific foreign policies, he would have been supportive, because they were, after all, his policies.

The State Department as an institution is an easy one to kick, and most presidents have from time to time kicked it undeservedly. When it comes to administrative reforms, however, that was not one of my greatest achievements. Reforming any institution of the U.S.

government is really a very difficult undertaking for someone from the outside who is only there for a brief period of time. The long-term employees wait you out, and when you are gone, it's right back to the same old ways.

One undertaking that particularly discouraged me involved the Foreign Service. Recruiting able young people into the Foreign Service is a terribly important thing for our country. We want a slice of the best people coming out of our educational system to become Foreign Service officers. The system of recruiting Foreign Service officers, however, is such that from the time the student takes the foreign service exam, it is more than 18 months before that individual is notified as to his or her admission to the Foreign Service. If students take the exam while they are seniors in college, they aren't notified for another year, so they take other jobs after they graduate, go on to graduate school, or choose another career. By the time they are notified, the best ones are already well-established doing something else. They were interested in an answer a year earlier. In the end, I reduced the time period to 12 months, but I couldn't reduce it to two months.

In the private sector we recruit many good people from our educational system, but there we can make decisions instantly, and if they are interested in working for our company, we can offer them a job that same day. I hear from friends that the time period for the government to offer a position is back to 18 months. The changes that we made have disappeared.

NARRATOR: There is a great tradition in American foreign policy in this country of people from Wall Street such as Paul Nitze, James Forrestal, John McCloy, and C. Douglas Dillon, who once in government have soon moved to the forefront of conducting day-to-day foreign policy. Sometimes when intellectuals cover the foreign policy problem, they leave out the chapter on contributions these people have made. John Whitehead is a classic example of someone who more recently became involved in U.S. foreign policy and who has done what McCloy and others did in an earlier period. We are all grateful and thank you very much.

CHAPTER 5

SERVING REAGAN AS NEGOTIATOR*

MAX M. KAMPELMAN

NARRATOR: Ambassador Kampelman has had a rich background in education, diplomacy, and law. In education, beginning with a bachelor's degree and a J.D. degree from New York University, and a master's and a doctorate from the University of Minnesota, he taught political science at the University of Minnesota, Harvard, Claremont, and Bennington. He has served as treasurer of the American Political Science Association. In the law field, he was for decades a partner in Fried, Frank, Harris, Shriver, and Kampelman.

In government, he was senior adviser to the U.S. delegation to the United Nations from 1966 to 1967 and held a series of appointments in the Reagan administration. He was ambassador and chairman of the U.S. delegation to the Conference on Security and Cooperation in Europe which met in Madrid from 1980 to 1983; co-chairman in 1984 of the U.S. delegation to observe the elections in El Salvador; ambassador and head of the U.S. delegation to the negotiations on nuclear and space arms from 1985 to 1989; and counselor of the Department of State since 1987.

He is the author of *The Communist Party vs. the CIO: A Study in Power Politics, The Strategy of Deception,* and *Three Years at the East-West Divide.* He moderated "Washington Week in Review" from 1967 to 1970.

Presented in a Forum at the Miller Center on 1 April 1989.

The selection that follows is part of a longer piece on "Negotiating with the Soviets." The excerpt for this volume begins with a response to a question on Gorbachev.

QUESTION: Given your statement of the principle of Soviet negotiation as extreme patience, the thoroughness with which they will study issues and the perception of the Soviet government as monolithic, it is intriguing to have Gorbachev come on the scene and see these dramatic new ideas rolling out of Moscow almost on a weekly basis. Obviously he is not participating in the negotiating process, so that may not be changing. But what impact is there in having a new leader who seems to be putting out these innovative ideas so rapidly in terms of the negotiations that are ongoing?

AMBASSADOR KAMPELMAN: It's a good question and it permits me to complete the circle because there are some changes that he has instilled. He is impatient with negotiating processes. He has indeed been rude to his negotiators. He doesn't understand why it takes so long, and that's quite different. I don't think these people ever had that kind of an experience with Andrei Gromyko.

In January of 1987 they brought in a new counterpart to me, again a deputy foreign minister—first deputy foreign minister—named Vorontsov, and he had lots of other things to do. I met him on 15 January 1987, at which time he said very candidly to me, "I've got other things to do; I'm handling the Gulf and Afghanistan. You can see that's a big agenda," which of course I recognized. "But," he said, "my government has asked me to come here to see what I could do about getting these negotiations moving. What suggestions do you have?" This was a very good, businesslike approach. I told him what suggestions I had, and then I told him that, as a matter of fact, I had not been quite sure they had serious negotiators for most of 1985 and 1986, which was accurate. I gave him suggestions that I had made that had been turned down. We called the rest of the negotiating team together for the next day and laid it out.

As of that time I was appointed also to serve as the Counselor to the State Department with arms negotiations being one of my responsibilities. He told me he could only be in Geneva maybe four or five times a year, although he said, "I'll be here as often as need be," so I said to him, "Look, I too am in a similar position. I have to be in Washington most of the time. Let's just agree that we both get back here periodically and that we both get back here at the same time," which we did. I think we got back five or six times in the course of the year to take inventory of what was happening during our absence. We tried to overcome some things and push things through a little bit further. Gorbachev had injected that.

When there were meetings between either Reagan and Gorbachev or Shultz and Shevardnadze, there was great pressure on the Soviet negotiators to have something to show. The Soviets like to have a statement come out of it showing movement at the conclusion of a high-level meeting. So this pressure was there to move a little faster.

Let me use Madrid as an example of a miscalculation, where patience hurt them. They were very eager to have the Madrid meeting come up with an agreement to hold another meeting among the 35 countries on military confidence-building measures, which they called a meeting on disarmament. We had accepted the French idea for such a meeting as well. The first decision made by Ronald Reagan as President was to support that French idea, which was a turning point because when Ronald Reagan became President, none of us really knew how he was going to feel toward NATO or toward our allies, and this was a pro-NATO decision. I think the fact that Al Haig was secretary of state at that point helped immensely in that move, and Reagan supported NATO.

Why did they want this meeting? I feel—and you are never really quite sure—that they were desperately trying to stop us from deploying the Pershings and cruise missiles on the mainland of Europe. They knew this was a hot political potato for the Germans, the Belgians, the Norwegians, the Danes, and the British. They felt that if an agreement would come out of Madrid to have what they would call a meeting on disarmament, even though it was a meeting on military confidence-building measures, that this would permit them to go to the publics in Europe and say, "Why are you putting in more American missiles which is confrontational at a time when we've now agreed to hold a meeting on disarmament?" A clever move on their part. I knew this and so frankly I was not in a hurry.

When I took this job, I asked Cy Vance how long I would be needed, and he said, "Three or four months." It lasted three years. However, the fact of the matter was, if there was going to be an agreement, I was not that much in a hurry, although it was going to take a long time, I knew. As usual, they were not in a hurry either. They stalled and stalled and stalled, and by the time they finally came to terms—which meant agreeing with us as they finally did—the die was cast on the Pershings and cruise missiles. They could no longer stop it. That was their miscalculation.

I think had they made the same concessions they made at the end at some earlier time, I would have been in a position of saying, "How could I not take the concessions?"

NARRATOR: Was Reykjavík as much of a disaster as Henry Kissinger claims it was?

AMBASSADOR KAMPELMAN: It was both a disaster and a breakthrough; it was both. The disaster was the realization that Ronald Reagan was prepared to go down to zero on all nuclear weapons, and this was a shocker to our European friends, as well as to many Americans. We still are experiencing some problems with our European friends on that realization. I want to add a word about that. Ronald Reagan is opposed to nuclear weapons. This was not something frivolous; this was not something he hadn't thought about; this was not something he got tricked into. The fact of the matter is he wants to go down to zero on nuclear weapons.

I can tell you for a fact that I don't know a single one of his advisers when he was President who agreed with him. I was present at meetings where rather polite issue was taken with him, in his presence, and he never budged on it.

Let me give you one response that I heard him give, which I thought was quite effective. I don't agree with him on the nuclear weapons going down to zero now, certainly not now. I suppose if all conventional weapons were reduced to infinitesimal proportions, it would be perfectly good for nuclear weapons to go down to zero. I remember his thought, "The Soviets had Chernobyl; we could have Chernobyl. Let's assume the next Chernobyl is not a power plant, but a nuclear weapon plant, and it is in the United States. Public opinion in the United States and public opinion throughout the West will lead us to get rid of these nuclear weapons, just as in the electric power area, where we are now at the point where except in France, negative public opinion makes nuclear power plant construction almost impossible. Look at what's happening to the American industry." Then he said, "At that point it will be unilateral disarmament. We will be the ones, the West will be the ones, pressed by public opinion to get rid of the nuclear weapons. The Soviets will not be restrained by that, given the fact they are increasing their nuclear energy in the power field; they are increasing while Europe is decreasing." So he continued, "Let's do this through negotiation instead of doing it by the inevitable accident requiring us to do it." That was an argument, which I must say to you, I had not thought of before, and which had some appeal to it. But that was the negative part of Reykjavík.

On the other hand, I will say to you that breakthroughs in many areas were very significant. The breakthroughs in INF and in START took place there. There were lots of agreements in principle that were later finalized or formalized.

I think, though, that Gorbachev and Reagan left very irritated with one another. As both thought about it, they appreciated that a great deal had been done, and both then began to talk about the pluses that came out of Reykjavík.

NARRATOR: Mr. Ambassador, the question we've asked everybody in the Reagan oral history has been: Were the institutional relationships about right as you saw them? Were your relations with the secretary the right kind of relationships? Did you have access to the President? Did you get support for your negotiating positions, in contrast to Paul Nitze, who did not get such support after the "walk in the woods"?

AMBASSADOR KAMPELMAN: You have to understand that I was not on the scene during the "walk in the woods." I didn't enter the scene, the disarmament scene, until 1985. I was in Madrid while Paul was talking INF, including the "walk in the woods," and as a matter of fact Paul and I both went to Bonn—I from Madrid, he from Geneva—to brief Chancellor Kohl on both of these negotiations at the same time. So I had a chance to talk to Paul and see where he was going. I'll speak only for myself, not for Paul.

I could not have had more access or better access than I had in Madrid and in Geneva. I have absolutely nothing to complain about in those areas. The Madrid access to Carter was clear, but it was only for a few months. The Madrid access to Reagan was somewhat accidental. I was at a conference on armaments in Munich, in the audience, when the head of the conference asked me if I would be willing to come up front and talk about the Madrid meeting, and I did. Present in the audience, although I did not know it, was the new national security adviser, Judge William Clark. At the end of my talk I went back to the rear, sat in my seat, and he came over to me. I'd never met him. He said, "Have you ever had a chance to discuss this with President Reagan?" I said, "No." Now you have to remember that he was new; this was early in the Reagan administration also, right after Dick Allen left. "Well," he said, "I'd like you to talk to the President about this. I think the President should hear what you have to say." I said, "I'd be delighted," so he arranged a meeting which turned out to be a seminar in the Oval Office. The President, Vice President Bush, Meese, Baker, Deaver—really the top people—Clark and McFarlane. We must have spent an hour and a half talking about the Madrid meeting and talking about the Soviets. That, of course, opened up a lot of doors as far as the President was concerned, and I did have perhaps three or four additional experiences with the President during the Madrid meetings.

For example, at one point—I'm thinking now of what would be useful for your study—I felt we would get an agreement. I didn't know how long it would take, but I felt the Soviets were going to give us what we needed. It might be, let's say, a year and a half before the meeting would be over. I just sensed that. By then Shultz was secretary of state. I said to Shultz, "Look, I think we are going to get an agreement. Does the President want an agreement?" It was a good question, because he'd never had an agreement with the Soviets before. Shultz said, "Haven't you ever asked him?" I said, "No, never quite in those words." He said, "Didn't you see him last week?" I said, "Yes, I did see him last week, but there were other people in the room, and I didn't feel I wanted to ask when there were other people in the room." He said, "Well, let's find out." He picked up the phone and within a few minutes we were over at the White House. He said, "Mr. President, Max has a question to ask you." I asked him the question, and I got the answer: "Sure I want an agreement, if it's our agreement. If it is an agreement in our interest, and if it's one that you and George are prepared to recommend, sure I want it."

At one point I became dissatisfied with our position, a position which I had formulated. In Madrid I wrote all the instructions from Washington to me. You have to understand that Washington did not think anything would come out of Madrid. The result was nobody paid any attention to what I was doing in Madrid. I wrote my own instructions. People knew me; I had a lot of friends—you know I'd been in Washington a long time—who had confidence in me. Nobody thought an agreement would come out of Madrid. So the attitude was, "Let Max do what he wants to do."

At one point after the meeting at which I asked, "Do you want an agreement, Mr. President?", I began to feel that what we were asking of the Soviets was not enough. For me it was not enough. We were asking for them to agree to certain important words, but I wanted certain people to be permitted to emigrate from the Soviet Union. At that point I was sufficiently irritated with the system, irritated with the Soviets, and fed up with the increasing inhumanity that I wanted them to say "Uncle," if I can use that word, and that meant I wanted people out of there.

This was not the position we had arrived at with NATO when we started the Madrid meeting. But you have to remember that when we started the Madrid meeting, it was based on an assumption that the rest of the West wasn't even fully certain we should be emphasizing human rights as much as we were. There was a previous meeting in Belgrade at which the United States was the only country to mention the names of the victims of Soviet repression, and the United States mentioned six names. Three years later the Madrid negotiations opened. I want to tell you that by the end of the Madrid meeting, I think 18 or 19 countries mentioned the names of the victims, which they had refused to do three years earlier, and I think more than 200 or 250 names were mentioned rather than the six. So there was a lot of movement in the human rights area. It was a united NATO group. When I mentioned my feelings to George Shultz, and I said that I was simply uncomfortable with it, personally, he said, "Well, we have to ask the President."

Incidentally, I want to say to you, since you are doing the Reagan oral history project, that as far as George Shultz was concerned, he was constantly saying, "I have to go talk to the President." If anybody misses that point, it is a mistake. As you know I was counselor to the State Department; I worked with George Shultz. There were four of us who met regularly: John Whitehead, Mike Armacost, myself, and Shultz, every single day on any issue, and Shultz constantly said, "Get a paper for me; I've got to take this up to the President." So in this case, we had to take this to the President. So I went to the President and told him that I felt we had to do to change our position. I also told him that none of our allies would be in favor of it. He said, "Do you have to tell them?" I said, "Well, I don't have to tell them that boldly, but I certainly have to tell you, and I have to know whether you are going to support me in this." There was no hesitation on his part to support me.

Sure enough when the Germans began to suspect the change, Chancellor Kohl got on the telephone, called Ronald Reagan, complained about the fact that I seemed to be exceeding the requests of the Soviets. I'm told by people who took notes—because Kohl doesn't speak English and Reagan didn't speak German, so we had people on the phone taking the notes—that Reagan was great about it. In fact, I saw the notes.

NARRATOR: There are two other questions we've asked everybody, one of which you may not want to discuss. What were the obstacles? The media has played up the divisions between Defense and State, particularly in the Weinberger era, and naturally that is one issue that we'd hoped to get into.

The other question is, what was your impression of the President? We've asked this in each of the oral histories. What was your impression of the President as a political leader at your first meeting? Did you modify that view in any way as you went along, and what do you think history's judgment is going to be of this President?

AMBASSADOR KAMPELMAN: Let me answer them in turn. Our interagency process is a cumbersome process, but it is a necessary process. It is particularly cumbersome when one of the important agencies is skeptical about the results and wonders whether there should be any result at all. In my opinion Cap Weinberger probably did not wish to have an arms reduction agreement, though I haven't the slightest doubt in my mind that Ronald Reagan did. Since Cap was a loyal Cabinet member, he was going to go along with what the President wanted. You can understand that with his mind-set, he couldn't conceive of an agreement that was in the U.S. interests. He felt that he could persuade the President when the time came that the agreement being talked about was not in the U.S. interest, and therefore he could handle it. That created lots of delays in our ability to come up with a U.S. position. So if you asked me what was the greatest problem, I would say this was it.

On the other hand, one could ask whether I would change the interagency system. Not a bit. I had an interagency system in Geneva. We had three negotiations running simultaneously: INF, START, and space. I was the head of the negotiations overall and I handled space. Each one of these three negotiating groups had representatives from five government agencies on it as members: State Department, Arms Control and Disarmament Agency, Joint Chiefs of Staff, Office of the Secretary of Defense, and the intelligence agencies. These were in addition to the National Security Council, or the White House, which was always present in all of these things, though not formally a delegate. So you see what a large group we had. We also had our own interagency group, and I insisted on that. They insisted as well; the President wanted it. We talked out these things among ourselves, you see.

Let me say to you, that I would not say the same thing about Richard Perle that I've just said about Cap. I believe Richard Perle *was* prepared to have an arms agreement, whereas I don't believe Cap was. Now Richard may tell you, "No, Cap wanted one, too, but it had to be in our interest," but I don't think so. I've talked enough with Cap to know.

Let me also say this about Richard Perle. When I got an agreement together in Madrid (and, as I indicated to you, nobody expected it), and the State Department saw there was an agreement, we then had to go to Defense to get approval. The people in the State Department said, "Defense won't accept the agreement; they don't want an agreement." I knew the decisionmaker for the Madrid meeting was Richard Perle, so I said, "Well, talk to them." "Oh, no, *we* are not going to talk to them," which was a foolish kind of thing for the particular head with whom I was speaking to say. He said, "*You* talk to them." So I said, "All right, I'll go see Richard." I dropped by his home on a Sunday, and we talked about the agreement. Richard said, "Max, do you think it's a good agreement?" I said, "It's a good agreement, Dick." So he said, "Let's go for it," just like that. He had confidence in me; he knew what we were doing and we did it.

First, let me tell you why I think Richard wanted an arms agreement: He wanted an arms agreement that he developed. By that I mean an agreement of which he knew the provisions, because he knew that *he* wasn't going to sell out the United States. He really was not sure about the next guy, particularly if the next guy was in the State Department, but he knew that *he* would not sell out the United States.

He and I used to talk about this. He saw an agreement under Ronald Reagan as a very rare opportunity to make profound worldwide political changes. For Ronald Reagan, with his talk of "evil empire" and "strong defense," to make the moves toward peace and to achieve something that nobody else could achieve, would in effect repudiate growing pacifism in the churches and growing pacifism in the leftist political parties, because none of them could achieve anything. It would also strengthen the Thatchers and the Kohls of this world because the conservatives could say, "We are the true peacemakers; we are negotiating from strength, which we have to do. We are negotiating from firmness. You have to understand the nature of the adversary." There is a tremendous political thrust to it, and Richard understood that.

Let me give you another illustration. John Warner of Virginia and Sam Nunn of Georgia came up with an idea for "nuclear risk reduction centers." I still do not fully understand how nuclear risk reduction centers are going to work, but it had a tremendous name, "risk reduction." I always used to feel the fellow who developed the concept of an "excess profits tax" was a genius—nobody can be against a windfall profits tax. Well, a "risk reduction center" has much of the same advantage. I attended many meetings at the White House when we were trying to figure out what this nuclear risk reduction center was, and what John and Sam had in mind. But they did have it in mind, and obviously, given the power these two capable people had in the Senate Armed Service Committee, nobody was going to be against it. They were both going to visit Gorbachev in Moscow. They asked, "How would you feel if we were to take this up with Gorbachev?" Everybody said, "Of course, let them take it up with Gorbachev." They thought, "Maybe he will kill it." They did take it up with Gorbachev, and Gorbachev thought it was great. Later we heard from the Soviets, "Gorbachev didn't quite understand what was meant by your two senators. Would you tell us what they had in mind?"

In any case, an agreement was made to negotiate nuclear risk reduction centers, and Sam and John both came to Geneva. They were both, I want to say, very serious, careful observers of our negotiations, and both were in Geneva many times. At one point, they were both as angry as can be, and they took me aside and said, "Max, we are just very upset. What do you advise us to do?" I said, "What's the problem?" They said, "Well, the problem is that the person chosen to negotiate the nuclear risk reduction for the United States is Dick Perle, and you know he is going to kill it." I said—and I think they were both surprised—"The best thing that could happen to you fellows is to have Dick Perle negotiate this treaty, because he will produce it, because he knows that what he comes up with will be good for the country. So don't be concerned about it. If somebody else were negotiating this, Dick would be against it." Well, you know that's exactly what happened. The Soviets, who thought of Richard Perle as some black demon, came over to me at the conclusion of very brief negotiations—it didn't take long—to say how impressed they were with Richard. So, anyhow, that's a long answer to your first question about the interagency process.

I do want to say, however, that there is another obstacle to the negotiations, which is that the United States simply still does not have a policy on mobile missiles; we still do not have agreement among ourselves on a land-based missile. The fight between the MX and the Midgetman or some alternative (or none of them at all) is still not resolved, and that is a barrier.

At one point somebody said to the President in my presence, "Mr. President, if Gorbachev came to you tomorrow and said, 'OK, we've got a lot done, but we've got a few things left; you write the treaty and I'll sign it,' Mr. President, we still couldn't write the treaty." That's part of our problem. There are still some questions—they are fewer in number now, and we are working them out, but we don't have everything yet in hand. That's obviously a handicap.

Now your other question has to do with my perception of the President. I don't know that I can see a difference between the President the first time I met him and the President the last time I met him, because the first time I met him in office was the seminar I mentioned to you which was a rather positive experience. It was an extraordinarily good meeting and he participated; he listened more than he spoke, but he participated; he was actively involved in it. I have always found him attentive and responsive.

Have I ever seen him nodding off? Yes, but I will confess to you that I have nodded off sometimes as well.

I remember being at a meeting in NATO after Moscow with George Shultz reporting, and I was sitting right in the front row, but in back of him. I kept awake while he was reporting, but when he had finished, all the other 15 had to make some comments, and I just kept nodding off; I couldn't keep my eyes open. I was tired after the Moscow trip. I stood up, left and came back, and still it was not enough. Anyhow, yes, I have seen the President nod off.

He does not have, in my opinion, a mastery of detail. I am impressed with his instincts, truly impressed with his instincts. He gets something in his head and it stays with him. We had lots of arguments around the table in his presence on the question of mobile missiles. The differences of the agencies would again be presented to him. The first time he listened to this and then said, "I just want to tell you how I feel about this." He said, "Let's assume we don't have an agreement with the Soviets on mobiles. Are we going to go ahead and build mobiles?   Is Congress going to give us the money we need for the Midgetman? The answer is probably no. Are the Soviets going to continue to build their mobiles? The answer is undoubtedly yes. We would then be disadvantaged. Why is it in our interest not to have limitations on mobile missiles? Why not have some mutual restraint?" It made sense to me.

A few months later we had the argument all over again. He repeated the same argument. Each time when he did this, this was, in effect, his decision. He had an instinct about these things; it was a political instinct, more than an instinct based on mastery of all of the facts, but the instinct was rather good.

There is another point in connection with that discussion I had with him about my wanting to get some people out. At the end of it he walked over to his desk, opened a drawer, took out a sheet of paper and gave it to me, and said, "Max, if you can, get these people out, too." I don't know how he got the names or why he had the names; obviously it was in his head. So I want to say to you that my general reaction to Reagan—and I speak to you as a Democrat—is a very positive one.

There is an article in the *National Interest* by a professor of political science at Berkeley, Aaron Wildavsky, on the Reagan presidency. It's a little early to express judgments about how history will resolve anything, but Aaron, at this early stage (and Aaron is also a Democrat), evaluates the Reagan presidency in extremely favorable terms. I think it is worthwhile for your study to look at Aaron's piece. It is a perceptive piece.

I would say one problem with the Reagan administration was its inability to work as closely with the Congress as I think they should have. I think, for whatever reasons, they simply did not take as much advantage of it as they should have and could have. I think more would have been accomplished had this thing been better executed.

QUESTION: Do you foresee the prospect of the Soviet Union being deloused, killing off the bugs, and knocking down barriers to people leaving the country, even if they don't decide to let everybody in?

AMBASSADOR KAMPELMAN: Gorbachev and those who support him know they have a failed system. It doesn't work. You know under the czars Russia exported food; today they can't feed their own people. The system is a failure. They know that. Their task is how to bring it into the modern era technologically, economically, and commercially. It is a very difficult task.

If I have any gifts, I know that prophesy is not one of them, so I'm hesitant to judge this. I know logically that they cannot do it. If I were betting, I would say they cannot do it. But I learned a long time ago that politics, including international politics, is not rational and not logical, and they might do it. I'm not yet prepared to bet that they won't do it.

They have to do it if they are going to survive as a system. They understand the need to humanize their system now, because they have been the pariahs of the world. They are in a situation where no people any place in the world would voluntarily subject themselves to their system, and they know that. That couldn't have been said 20 years ago. The acknowledgement of their failures and inhumanities is widespread. They know that; this is not a surprise to those who are intelligent about it, so they have to change the system.

They'd like to make as few changes as possible. The leaders look upon themselves as Leninists. We ought not to kid ourselves about that. They want to make as few changes as possible. They'll make as many as they have to and as few as they can get away with. That's Gorbachev's problem; what can he get away with as he makes these changes. There is tremendous resistance throughout the system.

You have brave, heroic, intellectual leaders saying fantastic things openly. You can speak to some of the maverick young lawyers, some not even so young, talking about the need to change their legal system. I had one lawyer say to me, "We made a mistake when we proceeded to adopt the Roman system. We should have gone to the Anglo-Saxon system. We would then know now how we can move to your system of law." They want to do that. This man said that he knows that at the Gorbachev level there is support, but between the Gorbachev level and his level, there is total opposition.

Let's take the case of psychiatric hospitals. A group of psychiatrists have just returned from a historic visit—I think they visited 11 or 15 Soviet psychiatric institutions that they selected. They made a point of not telling the Soviets which institutions until one week ahead of time, so they couldn't scrub them all in time. You do have a group of younger psychiatrists who have now formed an association who want to make changes, but at the levels in between there is resistance to the changes. The man who heads up the Ministry of Health (a man incidentally who hurt Sakharov and then as a leader of International Physicians for the Prevention of Nuclear War, received the Nobel Peace Prize in 1985—a shameful step in my opinion) is one of the fellows refusing to acknowledge the necessity for changes in the use of psychiatric hospitals for political punishment. This man, named Yevgeny Chazov, opposes these changes, yet he received a Nobel Peace Prize. He is the fellow who helped put Andrei Sakharov away and he gets the Nobel Peace Prize. When you think about it, you must be struck by the outrage of it. So you have this dichotomy: At the top level and among heroic people down below there are those who want to change it, but there is resistance in between. I don't know if it will work or not. My own opinion is that it is in our interest that it does work.

NARRATOR: Ambassador Kampelman continued this discussion about personalities and policy-making. By discussing Soviet policymakers, he helps illuminate the political environment in which Reagan and Gorbachev held discussions. On both sides there were many misunderstandings. By understanding the political environ-ment we can grasp a little more clearly the terrain along which President Reagan had to travel. Critics often forget the way in which this offered a far greater challenge taken up by the negotiators and in particular the leaders at the top, Reagan and Gorbachev.

CHAPTER 6

REAGAN'S LEADERSHIP: MYSTERY MAN OR IDEOLOGICAL GUIDE?*

ELLIOTT ABRAMS

NARRATOR: During his career Elliott Abrams has served at several levels of government. He began his career at Harvard where he earned the bachelor of arts and doctor of law degrees. He also received a masters of science degree in economics from the London School of Economics.

Mr. Abrams practiced law with the New York firm of Breed, Abbott and Morgan before becoming assistant counsel to the United States Senate Permanent Subcommittee on Investigations. He later served as special counsel to Senator Henry Jackson and as special counsel and chief of staff to Senator Pat Moynihan.

Following a brief return to the practice of law, he eventually joined the Reagan administration in three capacities: He first served as assistant secretary for international organization affairs in the Department of State, then as assistant secretary for human rights and humanitarian affairs, and finally as assistant secretary for Inter-American affairs. Since leaving the government he has been a senior fellow at the Hudson Institute in Washington, D.C., and is presently writing a book. It is appropriate as we explore the Reagan presidency through our oral history series that we visit with Secretary Abrams.

Presented in a Forum at the Miller Center on 16 November 1990.

MR. ABRAMS: Thinking about Reagan as President, I am reminded of a statement made by a State Department official, Tom Simons, who is now ambassador to Poland.   In his book, which concerns U.S. foreign policy in the 1980s, Simons calls Reagan a mysterious man, and I think there is a lot to that.   Reagan is mysterious both in certain personal ways and in terms of certain leadership qualities.

In attempting to isolate those qualities responsible for Reagan's success as President, I believe it is useful to suggest that he was a terrific president but not a terrific prime minister.   If our system were more like the French system, the administration probably would have functioned better.   Despite his eight years as governor of California and his eight years as President of the United States, Reagan was not a particularly good executive, and he would never have been chosen to serve as prime minister in such a system.

Reagan also had a different view of what the presidency requires, one that I believe is closer to the truth.   He viewed the presidency as not simply an executive position but also as an inspirational position.   As a head of state, the President was a symbolic leader of the people rather than simply a manager of the government's institutions.   Reagan filled the first role much better than he did the latter.

NARRATOR: How much contact did those of you at the assistant secretary level have with the President?

MR. ABRAMS: As one of the State Department's five regional assistant secretaries, I had a reasonable amount of contact with him, probably because Central America was so hot.   In 1986 and 1987 in particular, I generally met with the President a couple of times a week.   I never met alone with him, however, and I don't think many people at my level did.

In 1988 we did have a lot of meetings concerning Central America and, later on, Panama.   There were National Security Council (NSC) meetings, which I attended with Secretary of State Shultz, as well as what were known as National Security Planning Group meetings, which were at a higher level and which I also attended with Shultz.   We also had lobbying meetings where the President would lobby the Senate or House leadership or several members of Congress. Additionally, there were briefings, state visits, pre-briefs for the state visit, dinners, and lunches. In sum, there were an awful lot of meetings, probably at least two a week.

NARRATOR: Did the President ever fall asleep in any of the meetings that you attended?

MR. ABRAMS: No, but he was talking in those meetings, and it is difficult to fall asleep when you are actually speaking.

NARRATOR: Did the President take a very active part during those meetings?

MR. ABRAMS: It varied. I suppose the height of his participation concerned Central America and Panama issues, which he cared deeply about. There were some meetings where he led the conversation and held a very strong position—for instance, on Panama—even though he had not been briefed. He knew what he thought, and he argued articulately with, say, James Baker on an issue. On the other hand, there were meetings with foreign leaders, for example, where the President was not familiar with the issues and the Cabinet essentially carried the conversation. Why anyone would expect that a president should be deeply familiar with our economic concerns in Uruguay is beyond me, however.

NARRATOR: You mentioned Panama. Why was that a problem for Reagan?

MR. ABRAMS: Panama is an interesting issue in the context of the Reagan presidency because it gave rise to some very good as well as some not so good moments for the President. Taking the good first, I don't think I ever saw him better in terms of knowledge of the issue, energy, engagement, intelligence, and concern than he was over the question of whether we should quash the indictment of General Noriega. You may recall that in the spring of 1988 we were negotiating to remove General Noriega from power. It was clear that he would not go unless the indictments were quashed, and the argument in favor of doing so was that the indictment itself was simply a piece of paper and was not useful. If it could be traded to get Noriega out of Panama, however, that would be terrific.

One argument against quashing the indictment was that it would constitute a dirty deal with a drug dealer and would be a terrible blow to our entire drug program. Moreover, such a deal would not be good for the Bush campaign. There was much argument on this issue, some of it very emotional, but ultimately the argument was between Secretary Baker speaking for Bush and the President speaking for himself. I never saw the President more aware of all sides of an argument and more certain of his point of view.

On the negative side, I would generally say that the Reagan administration at least in terms of foreign policy was an administration in which contentious issues were settled at the Cabinet level. I remember John Negroponte, the deputy national security adviser at that time, saying at the end of one contentious session in the White House situation room that they could not take the issue to the President but had to resolve it themselves. I remember thinking then: What does the President get paid for? Why did the Cabinet have to resolve it? Let the President resolve it.

That, however, was not the way things were done. Rather, if two Cabinet officers were not able to resolve a question, they would wrangle and wrangle, and there was never closure. That is what happened with the Panama issue. Everybody agreed that Noriega should be confronted and indicted, and everybody agreed that his firing of President Eric Delvalle in late February 1988 was unacceptable. All agreed that we would challenge him and use tough rhetoric. When it came time to do something, however, the State Department was ready to act, but the Defense Department was not, and the President did not adjudicate the question. During meeting after meeting of the National Security Council (NSC) or the National Security Planning Group, things became pretty nasty between Secretary Shultz and Frank Carlucci or between Shultz and Admiral William Crowe in particular, but the President wouldn't say anything.

Another theory with which I don't agree but which is plausible is that the President actually agreed with the Pentagon on inaction but did not want to say to his secretary of state, "You lose." Therefore he temporized, and as time went by and no action was taken, the Pentagon won by default. This was a case where both the military and the State Department had strong arguments, and the President was virtually immobilized by an extremely tough fight among his trusted Cabinet officers. In that sense, the Panama issue pointed to a difficulty in the policy-making apparatus.

NARRATOR: One of your colleagues mentioned that on issues of particular concern to him—and I think he referred to Panama—President Reagan did an enormous amount of homework. He also noted that earlier on several issues in California Reagan had burned the midnight oil to master the details. Would that distinguish the President's mode of operation on Panama from his handling of other issues?

MR. ABRAMS: I was not really in a position to judge that, but to the extent that I could, I would disagree. What changed with respect to Central America or Panama was that while the President's memory was selective and he didn't remember things that he didn't care about, in those two cases he remembered everything he was told.

I remember anecdotes that I told him about Central America which he repeated to a congressman three months later. When he cared, he absorbed everything and could turn around and repeat a briefing that he had received. However, I do not believe that he was sitting around at night reading histories of Panama.

QUESTION: We have heard from several people that the Cabinet didn't really function as a Cabinet in a conventional sense. Apart from the secretary of defense, the secretary of state, and the secretary of the treasury, the rest were more or less honorary jobs with little working function or responsibility outside each respective department. Would you agree?

MR. ABRAMS: Yes, although my perspective was from the State Department, and I don't know how housing or economic policy was handled, for example. I don't know what the roles of the commerce secretary and the U.S. trade representative were. Certainly in terms of the foreign policy process, those individuals had no role.

COMMENT: I've always found it surprising that we would indict Noriega, a foreign head of state, who had not even been in this country. Although under our law we were supposed to try him, I'm assuming that there was much legal and political argument against the indictments. However, as you also suggested, after the indictments were brought, there was a great deal of concern that dismissing them might have unfortunate political repercussions for Vice President Bush.

MR. ABRAMS: First, I don't think there were any legal difficulties involved. Noriega was periodically in the United States, and under the classic long-arm idea of criminal jurisprudence, an individual might be held liable even if he has not set foot in a state.

Politically, this issue raises other questions. Generally speaking, we do not indict foreign leaders for the same reason that we don't assassinate foreign leaders. Once one starts down that road, there are going to be regrets and worries about the ability of the president himself to travel.

We issued the indictment anyway, for a mixture of reasons. First, we reasoned that Noriega was not an elected leader and not the president of Panama. In fact, at no time did he even claim to be president of Panama. Although he was a high foreign official, he was not a head of state and therefore did not qualify for the head of state exception. Moreover, we believed that he was a criminal. We were pursuing him not for a crime tinged with politics (e.g., holding political prisoners or not allowing for a free press) but rather for a purely criminal act—drug trafficking. However, there were also politics involved in the decision. Washington did not invent the idea of indicting Noriega. Rather, it was invented by two U.S. attorneys in Florida whom we—at least those of us in the State Department—suspected of wanting to be the next governor of Florida. Anyway, once somebody suggests indicting Noriega, there is a problem. No one wants to be the guy whose name appears on the front page of the *Washington Post* the next day for having said no to the indictment. We held a meeting on this issue with a number of individuals, including representatives from the State and Defense departments and the CIA, and noted that the indictment would go through unless someone objected. No one did, however, and it occurred to me as I was sitting there that some of the people who might actually have thought the indictment was a dumb idea were not raising their hands because they were afraid of leaks.

So we went ahead and indicted Noriega, and then we had an entirely new problem. Here, I think, there was a mistake made on my part as well as that of others in the administration. I did not believe that the indictment itself would become an issue in American politics or a big deal in the Reagan administration. I thought that the indictment would simply serve as a bargaining chip and that when it came time to get Noriega out of Panama, we could quash the indictment if we were not able to do anything with it. As it turned out, the indictment had a life of its own and became a big political factor. The argument was that quashing the indictment would undercut the entire antidrug program and that people, believing Noriega had information about the vice president's role, would accuse him of a cover-up. So, we erred in not anticipating that this matter would become a domestic political issue.

I remember that Richard Cheney, who was then a congressman from Wyoming, told me that everyone in Wyoming was against quashing the indictment. When I asked why, he answered that who rules Panama is of relatively little significance to people in Wyoming. Dealing with drug dealers and quashing U.S. indictments, on the other hand, was of concern.

In the end, though, the President decided he would nullify the indictment. It was only because Noriega would not make an agreement with us that this action was not taken. In fact, the President, after a long argument, had overruled the vice president and Baker and Meese as well. He was willing to take that action if that was what it would take to get rid of him.

QUESTION: I believe that when Jean-Claude Duvalier was ousted as president of Haiti, the United States was able to lean on the French and convince them to grant asylum to Duvalier without much difficulty. Did you have trouble getting the Spaniards to accept Noriega?

MR. ABRAMS: The French agreed to take Duvalier temporarily with the understanding that the United States would assist in finding permanent asylum for him. In fact, the United States conducted an unbelievable survey. I believe we asked about 30 countries to take Duvalier off the hands of the French. Nobody would do it, so there he sits. The Noriega case, however, was easy. Oddly enough, the Spanish came to us. Toward the end of summer 1987, before Noriega was indicted but after it had become clear that relations with him were worsening, a representative of Felipe Gonzalez's office who was in Washington at the time announced that the Spanish would take him. He noted that Spain had a tradition of aiding democracy in Latin America by taking dictators off the hands of the Latin American people. They had taken Fulgencio Batista and Juan Peron and believed this was a contribution they could make.

Noriega would not go, however. He was the problem, not the Spanish. While we were negotiating with him, he ruled Spain out on the grounds that he didn't know anyone there and that it was too far from Panama. Apparently he wanted to go to the Dominican Republic, where he had a daughter who had married a Dominican general and where he owned property, but we didn't want him to take refuge so close to Panama.

QUESTION: President Reagan seems to have been as interested in the contras in Nicaragua as he was in Panama. To what extent would you say that the Iran-contra situation was influenced by the Reagan administration's desire to obtain money for the contras, and to what extent was it influenced by the desire to accomplish diplomatic progress in the Middle East?

MR. ABRAMS: Let me start with a comment I think is quite debatable. It seems to me that one of the greatest mistakes of the Reagan administration in its eight years was to try to achieve its goals in Nicaragua on the cheap. Even before he became President, Reagan was determined that we were not going to accept the Sandinistas' control as permanent; it would have been the equivalent of another Cuba. First, we were going to stop the Faribundo Martí National Liberation Front (FMLN) in El Salvador, and second we were going to do something about the Sandinistas. We were going to get them one way or another.

Although I am speaking from hindsight, I think the administration made a huge mistake by diving under on this issue instead of confronting Congress and public opinion. Stage one of this process was the administration's turnover of the problem to the CIA. Stage two occurred when the administration was forced to dive deeper because of the Boland amendment and use an organization that was theoretically more secret than the CIA, one that was off the books. The administration's handling of this problem, however, would have been flawed even if it had stopped with turning the problem over to the CIA. It was a mistake to define something as a very important security matter and then do it covertly. If Central America is important to our security, as the President repeatedly said it was, then it deserved not to be shunted aside as a matter for 30 guys in the CIA to handle.

For me, one of the great mysteries of the Reagan administration is what precisely Director of Central Intelligence William Casey's role was in all of this. When the buildup began in Nicaragua in October 1986, we had $100 million and began to build an army, which ultimately involved approximately 20,000 men. I remember telling Secretary Shultz right in the beginning that this was a mistake. The CIA does not know now to run armies. It had become a military rather than a covert operation and should have been run by our army. With 20,000 men, there are serious logistical problems which hundreds of colonels have made their life's work to learn how to handle.

I went on and on with what I thought was an extremely persuasive argument, comparing the strengths and weaknesses of the two institutions. When I finished, however, Secretary Shultz smiled and said, "Yeah, but Cap [Caspar Weinberger] won't touch it with a ten-foot pole, and Bill Casey wants it, so that is how it is going to be." That is political science at work!

As for the relationship between the North and Casey operations, I don't believe the two were initially linked. There was a belief at that time that we should pursue a relationship with Iran. This view was held by a number of people such as Donald Fortier, then deputy national security adviser. Fortier believed that we were tilting too far to Iraq, and from a November 1990 perspective, I think he was clearly correct. That tilt was not in the long-term strategic interest of the United States; we should instead have attempted to redress the balance. Fortier, however, developed cancer and died at age 42. Had he lived, our dealings with Iran might have been more successful.

At the same time, there was also a desire to keep the contras going. After the congressional funding cutoff, a number of ways of providing aid were explored. One of the legally authorized ways was to persuade some foreign governments to give money, as the Saudis had already done. I do not believe the link between the secret Iran effort and the contras was part of the original plan, and I don't know who connected the two. North claims that he did, but

Casey may also have been responsible. The two projects, however, would have existed even without that link.

QUESTION: Since World War II some of our presidents have had difficulty differentiating for the American public our political and military policy. Would you care to hazard a few comments on that?

MR. ABRAMS: One explanation for the manner in which our presidents have typically handled that question concerns the gap between the world role that our policy of containment has prompted us to play and the role the American people have been willing to accept. Originally our policy was sold as a cheap policy. For example, Dean Acheson, testifying before the Senate in 1947, was asked whether we would have a permanent troop presence in Europe. His response was, absolutely not; that was not even contemplated.

Initially the heart of our plan for Europe was the Marshall Plan. The military aspect was not incorporated until later. The containment policy was thus not supposed to require a large army or wars. Moreover, every time the containment policy got us into a war, there was an almost Newtonian reaction against it. For example, what evolved from the reaction to Korea was not only the defeat of the Democrats but also the doctrine of massive retaliation, which allowed the president to say that we were going to stop communism without any soldiers getting hurt. I think this was an effort to match the requirements of our containment policy with the reluctance of the American people to become involved in fights all over the place.

The same thing might be said of the Nixon Doctrine, which in a sense was a reaction to Vietnam. Since Vietnam also destroyed a presidency, how the president would deal with the Soviet menace and containment became a difficult issue. In the end, the shah was viewed as a way of handling the problem and preventing further wars.

The Reagan Doctrine essentially served the same purpose. Reagan believed that the Soviets had made significant advances in the late 1970s, in Nicaragua, Afghanistan, and Angola. In these cases, we avoid sending Americans to fight by supporting the contras, Jonas Savimbi in Angola and the Afghan rebels. Our efforts were directed not at raising the level of public willingness to engage in military action but at persuading the public that we could accomplish everything we needed to accomplish without it.

NARRATOR: To what extent might President Reagan's domestic political success in California, where he had proven his political mettle against an opposition legislature, have led him to believe that there were also ways of finessing foreign policy endeavors to avoid paying the maximum price?

MR. ABRAMS: Although I was not with Reagan in California, judging from what I have seen, he came to Washington with a negative view of the legislative branch in terms of foreign policy. Reagan was also reluctant to spend political capital. This was particularly visible in the 1984 campaign, when many Republicans questioned whether the President's goal was to achieve a landslide victory or to advance certain policy views. He was reluctant to take actions with clear political costs.

QUESTION: The Reagan administration was always critical of the link that was made between human rights and military aid. With Violeta Chamorro's rise to power in Nicaragua, do you think it is now more feasible to make that link with respect to El Salvador and Guatemala?

MR. ABRAMS: First, I would disagree with your premise that the administration always took the view that human rights and military aid should not be linked. We did view that issue differently than did the Carter administration. In some cases, we believed that they had insisted on the link for symbolic purposes, forgetting that some of the countries in question faced truly difficult military situations. To some degree our position was validated when, during the last three weeks of his administration, Carter resumed shipping arms to the Salvadoran junta—one of the least attractive governments at that time—because they desperately needed them.

Second, I would say that the administration's policy changed. There really was no human rights policy the first year. In terms of human rights, the Ernest Lefever hearings, which went on for several months, left the administration in disarray and with no one in the position of assistant secretary for human rights and humanitarian affairs. There was also a sort of visceral feeling on the part of some people—maybe the President and certainly Jeane Kirkpatrick—that the human rights initiative was bad and invented by the Democrats and that the Reagan administration was not going to have any part of it.

It took two players to achieve any kind of human rights policy in the administration. The first was me, and the second was George Shultz. I became assistant secretary for human rights and humanitarian affairs in December 1981, but it took us a while to get our doctrine straight. In fact, my deputy, Charles Fairbanks, who is now at Johns Hopkins, and I first had to write it. We had to figure out what a Reaganite human rights policy would look like in terms of dealing with Chile, Paraguay, South Africa, Korea, and Turkey. Our second obstacle, however, was that then Secretary of State Alexander Haig wasn't much interested in human rights. I may be being slightly unfair to him, but I believe that he viewed human rights as a rather foolish subject.

NARRATOR: Didn't Haig say that fighting terrorism was a better alternative?

MR. ABRAMS: Yes, he did. His thinking on the subject was not clear at all, and his attitude was basically negative. Shultz, however, had a very different and essentially nonideological view of human rights. His thoughts were that of course we were for human rights, and he approached the problem by asking us precisely what we would like done in a particular case and whether that action would be reasonable. Shultz arrived during the summer of 1982, and by the end of that year the human rights bureau was in business. Having the ear of the secretary of state constituted a big change for us.

NARRATOR: We have had people here representing different views, and no one has been critical of your tenure in the human rights bureau. Could you tell us a little bit more about how you functioned there? Who were your allies, and what did the President think about human rights?

MR. ABRAMS: We started from scratch in the sense that the bureau was in complete disarray when I arrived. Within the State Department, the important bureaus are the regional ones, while the functional bureaus—drugs, the United Nations, human rights, and economic—have a hard time gaining any territory. The human rights bureau was probably the weakest of all.

The first thing we did was recruit some good people for the bureau and formulate our positions. We wrote some essays and cables, some theoretical and some based on cases that existed in Poland. In 1982, Turkey, Central America, and Chile were all important in terms of human rights as well. Once Shultz became secretary, it became possible to make an argument in terms of human rights.

Generally, nations are divided into two groups: those that are relatively unimportant and thus fall under the policy jurisdiction of the State Department, and those in which other agencies have a say. For example, policies toward Chile, Paraguay, and Haiti are State Department managed, while Panama and the Philippines were also handled by the Department of Defense. In some locations, the Treasury Department also had a lot to say.

As for countries that we considered in our jurisdiction, we had to persuade only Shultz of our strategy. In Chile, the development of our human rights policy began with our telling Shultz that we believed there should be a greater distancing from, and opposition to, President Augusto Pinochet. One point that I do want to make is that when a new secretary comes in, all that is needed is to win one or two battles. After that, however, it is understood that you don't elevate every issue to the secretary; rather, you bargain about the text of cables and conditions and so forth. That is how matters were handled with Shultz.

As for the President's role, the President instantly grasped the desirability of an active, positive human rights policy. What he did not like, however, was the constant criticism of people who for the most part were pro-American. He did not mind criticizing Castro, but in dealing with countries such as Korea and Turkey, it displeased him to have to do so.

What the President liked very much and recognized the value of, whereas a lot of people who should have known better did not, was the idea behind the National Endowment for Democracy—that is, that it was important to aid the evolution of democracy. Doctrinally, we argued that we should move from case work, from trying to get Mr. A out of jail or reopening newspaper B to fostering systemic change. Only systemic change would guarantee that the one or two gains you had made would remain and that all political prisoners would be freed.

This strategy fit nicely with the President's instincts. He did not want to be smacking his friends all the time, but he did want to figure out a way to help. This was reflected in the President's speech to Westminster, which was written by Mark Palmer, former ambassador to Hungary, and which served as the beginnings of the National Endowment for Democracy.

President Reagan did not intervene in human rights policy often, but one did have to take into account what would happen if an issue were elevated to his level. The best example concerns Chile. We had what we thought was a very good policy about Chile. However, General Vernon Walters, then our U.N. ambassador, argued that we were being too critical of Pinochet and threatened to take things to the President. On several occasions we had to compromise because we were just not sure.

I was not at this meeting, but my deputy for South America did attend. The President suggested at one point in the discussion that if we could just talk to Pinochet, maybe we could get him to change some of his ways and then perhaps we should invite him to Washington. At that point, Shultz apparently vaulted out of his seat and said, "Don't even think about it!"

In sum, on the positive approach toward human rights, the President was gung-ho. In terms of the negative approach, however, he was dubious, and we had to be careful that we were not getting out in front of him.

Our worst failure in the human rights bureau concerned the Philippines. Apparently it pained the President to have to tell Ferdinand Marcos to go, since early on he had been a great friend. In fact, in approximately 1984 Marcos made a state visit to Washington, and I do not believe the term *human rights* was ever mentioned in the President's remarks. Reagan didn't want to have a difficult time with his friend.

NARRATOR: Is it possible, as U.S. ambassador to Chile Harry Barnes has argued, that pushing human rights worked in Chile because there that struggle could be linked to the struggle for freedom, which the President fervently believed in, whereas that link was more difficult to make in other places such as the Philippines?

MR. ABRAMS: While I think there is some element of truth to that, I would tend to disagree. Even though Pinochet claimed that chaos would follow an end to military rule, that was a foolish argument, and no one who really understood Chile believed it. In the Philippines it was easier to argue that the Marcos government could not be followed by real democracy. However, I think the basis of the President's strategy was more personal. Reagan believed that the Carter administration had beat up on American friends. Not only was that bad theoretically, but Reagan knew some of those people. Pinochet and he had never met, but he knew and presumably liked Marcos. He did not want to sour his relationship with Marcos by harping on human rights.

NARRATOR: Was Weinberger an ally on human rights?

MR. ABRAMS: I suppose that if we had tried to push hard against militarily important countries such as Turkey and the Philippines and had gotten past the White House, we would have encountered the Defense Department. In fact, that did happen in Panama. When we started to push against Noriega in 1985, it was the Defense Department that blocked our effort.

QUESTION: How would you contrast the Bush administration with the Reagan administration policy in terms of our Latin American policy? Bush traveled to South America during the first week of December [1990] to meet with the Argentine and Brazilian presidents, and it seems his administration's emphasis is on economic integration and free trade issues.

MR. ABRAMS: I see a sharp distinction between the policies of the two administrations primarily because it is a different world. Reagan assumed office when the Central American situation was terribly difficult. Jimmy Carter had torn apart and thrown away his entire Latin American policy during his last weeks in office by aiding the Salvadoran junta and cutting aid to the Sandinistas.

We believed we faced some serious security issues in the Caribbean Basin. First, we wanted to stop the fall of El Salvador, and second we were faced with Grenada, which at that time was led by Maurice Bishop and heading into trouble. We did not want another Nicaragua. Remember, in 1980 the Soviets had been enjoying a pretty good period. Furthermore, Mexico was not in good shape. Mexico was being run by a thief who was destroying the economy and who was not the first person to meet those qualifications. In sum, the entire region seemed very troublesome from a security point of view, and since security was our main concern, we paid more attention to the Caribbean Basin than we did to South America.

By the time Bush came in, however, those problems had passed; the security problem was declining. It was therefore possible for the President to turn toward what logic would suggest and what Reagan had understood: Mexico was critical. The Reagan administration had paid a lot of attention to Mexico. The trouble is that when Mexico is headed in the wrong direction, there is almost nothing we can do about it. When Mexico heads in the right direction, on the other hand, we can begin to help. In fact, when Carlos Salinas and Miguel de la Madrid asked for help, they received a fair amount. Bush has built on that, and he has built a terrific relationship with Salinas, which was a very smart thing to do.

Another smart thing Bush did was to ask where the people and the money are. The answer is: in South American countries such as Brazil, Argentina, Venezuela, and Colombia. Bush thus built personal relationships with the presidents of some of those countries and began to pay somewhat greater attention to South America. This could only be done after the situation closer to home was essentially in hand, although much attention was paid to Panama until the situation there was resolved.

One caveat, however, is that there is less to these relationships than meets the eye. If you were to talk to Venezuelan President Carlos Andrés Perez, you would find that he did not believe himself to be a great friend of President Reagan but does regard himself as a great friend of President Bush. You have to be a pretty cynical Washington-dweller to use the term *friend* to describe the relationship between the President and any Latin leader. Bush does have a much better style than Reagan did in dealing with many of the Latin presidents. He gives them a warm and appreciated feeling, which is politically quite useful.

As for what we are actually doing for Venezuela, however, the answer is not much. There is some question as to how much the Brady Plan, which was invented by the Reagan administration to reduce Latin American debt, has accomplished. The test will be whether the Initiative for the Americas program takes off over the next several years, particularly if President Bush has two terms. It is striking to me that you can search the *New York Times* and *Wall Street Journal* every month and find little mention of the Initiative for the Americas. However, it is daily fodder in the Latin press. They think and care about it, and if the President can build on that interest to obtain trade agreements, that will be a historic accomplishment. In sum, however, a North American free trade zone and the opportunity to concentrate on Mexico and South America have required prior resolution of security issues. Reagan dealt with those, and Bush has intelligently built on his efforts.

QUESTION: What do you think the political impact of the absence of a military draft has been on our foreign policy? Does its absence explain the comparatively little agitation and controversy about our buildup in the Gulf?

MR. ABRAMS: The impact of the all-volunteer military is hard to measure, but it seems that it may render the use of force easier for presidents by diminishing the domestic debate about that decision.

This gives me a chance, however, to note that Reagan was not much of a guy for using force. It is odd that he had the image of a tough guy who carried a big stick; yet, in terms of actually using force, he was quite careful. He did opt to use force in Grenada, which was a one-day deal, but he refused to do so in Panama, even though it would not have been that large of an operation. In part, Reagan may have been scared off by what happened in Beirut, which was such a disaster and tragedy, but I'm struck by the fact that he was really quite loathe to use the American military. As to why, I can only make two guesses: One concerns his temperament—he did not like sending people off to die—and the second, his advisers, on whom he relied a great deal. Weinberger, as you may recall, invented a set of rules that would have made it difficult to have conducted the American Revolution.

Admiral Crowe was also extremely cautious in terms of using military force and may be the single largest reason no action was taken in Panama during the Reagan administration. The President valued and listened to his advisers and the fact that his key military advisers were against using force had a large impact on his record also.

QUESTION: In hindsight, what are your views on the Panama Canal treaty?

MR. ABRAMS: I have very mixed views. Emotionally, I still don't like it. On balance, however, it was probably the right thing to do, and it will turn out all right. I do not take it for granted that we are going to give the canal back to Panama. Certainly if they get themselves another Noriega we will not, regardless of who is president. Suppose the canal agreement had been a ten- instead of a twenty-year treaty. Those ten years would have been up in the middle of Noriega's rule, and we would not have turned the canal over to him.

The treaty, however, does give the Panamanians an incentive to develop a calmer and more democratic political order, and it gives us the incentive to help them. One factor influencing both Reagan and Bush with respect to Panama—particularly Bush—was that as we approached the date for turning the canal over, we needed to prepare a decent and democratic government in Panama to take it. I would bet that over the course of the second ten years, that will happen, and I believe that the Panamanians will run the canal reasonably well when they do acquire it.

Actually, what I would like to see is some type of public corporation in which the Panamanian government owns only 51 percent of the canal, in which the Japanese and United States would invest. In that way the canal might be run on a more independent, nonpolitical, and commercial basis.

QUESTION: Regarding your comments on the Reagan Doctrine as containment on the cheap, conventional wisdom would suggest that Reagan's defense policy was anything but containment on the cheap. Do you think there were two tracks to his containment policy, one for the Third World and another for East-West relations?

MR. ABRAMS: No, I don't. In American political terms, building up your military defenses is cheap politically. Carter's projected budgets had also called for a significant military buildup. There was consensus on the Hill that we had to do something, although obviously not as much as Reagan wanted. Reagan did push up the totals a lot, but that action cost him little in terms of domestic political popularity. Dead soldiers, on the other hand, constitute a serious matter politically as well as morally. Thus, I would say that big military budgets are a cheap method of containment.

With respect to the Soviets, I think Reagan implemented this strategy with some malice aforethought. The idea was to spend the Soviet Union into the ground, and it worked. The plan was defensive in the sense that the Soviets had been spending a lot, and we needed to improve the readiness of our military. It was also based on the premise that in the spending race the Soviets were going to go under, although I don't know that anybody really believed that they would go under quite as dramatically as they have. In sum, the idea was to get somebody else to do our fighting for us.

By the way, I don't think it is at all surprising that there is currently a complete vacuum in terms of explanations for our handling of Iraq. According to my theory, we have been trying to run our security policy on the cheap for decades, but now that the Cold War is over, thousands of people may have to die, and it isn't even a matter of fighting the Russians.

QUESTION: Do you think the Bush defense policy—a policy under which I think we are going to see some cutbacks in terms of what we are willing to pay for defense, but under which we may end up by paying more in terms of lives—is a reaction to Ronald Reagan's defense policy in terms of the monetary costs?

MR. ABRAMS: I don't think so. The Bush administration faces a different problem than the Reagan administration did. The old bipolar structure assigned everybody a place, and every position was relative to the two superpowers. There were constraints on the actions of all other players because of their relationships with the superpowers. Now that the structure has collapsed, however, the security problems are coming from minor countries. In a sense, this is a new situation. During the American Revolution, we worried about the British, French, and Spanish empires, which were then the most powerful forces in the world. In the 19th century, Germany and Japan were growing in power, and in the 20th century the Soviet Union was. That is what we worried about, the most powerful countries.

Now, however, we do not worry much about the most powerful countries. We are not going to have a war with the Soviets or with the Germans or Japanese. Instead, we worry about relatively minor countries, which we don't quite know how to deal with yet. One mistake the Reagan administration made was to let Iraq become so heavily armed, although I also think that it was a tremendous diplomatic failure on the part of the Bush administration to have given Iraq the impression that it could take Kuwait for free.

QUESTION: I don't remember hearing much in the first half of the 1980s about how the defense buildup was intended to put pressure on the Soviet economy. Was that idea articulated in any way in the public arena? As a corollary to that point, I don't believe the U.S. government accepted the estimates of many persons in the private sector as to how weak the economy of the Soviet Union actually was.

MR. ABRAMS: I think you are right on both points. It is an interesting question as to why the U.S. government estimates on the Soviet economy, particularly those of the CIA, were so positive. I don't think anybody expected that we could spend the Soviets into oblivion. Rather, when the argument for increased defense spending was made, people would say that if we spent a lot and they matched our increases, it would hurt them more because they were poorer than we are.

The argument in the early 1980s, however, was a preparedness argument. In fact, about two weeks ago I heard a speech by Caspar Weinberger in which he reviewed this subject and noted that we had all sorts of equipment that didn't work and no spare parts; we were not militarily prepared. That was the main gist of the argument.

NARRATOR: If you were framing an oral history, what questions would you ask Weinberger and Shultz about their relationship?

MR. ABRAMS: In the human rights bureau we did not see much of Weinberger. It was clear, however, that the relationship between him and Shultz was poisonous; there was no hiding that fact. Given who was president and the collegial nature of the group, they actually crossed the line into direct face-to-face impoliteness, something that generally does not happen in presidential Cabinets.

The sarcasm and body language they used toward each other made you not want to get between the two of them. Their staffs essentially carried on this fight, committing guerrilla warfare against each other.

I believe things broke down because of that animosity. Since the President didn't enjoy adjudicating between two people he liked and trusted and would not side with one or the other, there were many standoffs on various matters. It would be interesting to explore the impact of their relationship on the national security advisers and vice versa. Looking back, I am struck by the weakness of some of Reagan's national security advisers, particularly since he was a president who relied on his advisers.

I can understand Bush having a weak national security adviser. If he said, "I know this stuff, this is my field, and I can do this," it might be wrong, but it wouldn't be shocking. In Reagan's case, however, it is quite surprising that he would have a weak national security adviser.

As a result, the Cabinet secretaries took over. In fact, from the beginning it was clear that Alexander Haig regarded National Security Adviser Richard Allen as someone who was there to be destroyed. There was not to be an independent foreign policy voice in the White House.

The system worked, however, with Colin Powell. To the extent that he gave an independent view, he did so very carefully, without offending the secretaries. The system required somebody of enormous bureaucratic skill in that position, and the other guys, with the possible exception of Frank Carlucci, did not have it. Although the system certainly did grind up national security advisers, at the same time, the people who where chosen for that job were generally not in a position to solve what I believe was a significant problem in the administration.

One example of the animosity between Shultz and Weinberger concerns the peace plan agreed upon by the Sandinistas and other Latin American presidents that did not involve the contras. I remember sitting in Shultz's office with him and Phillip Habib, reading the plan. I thought it was awful, but Phil liked it, and when we got to the last page he said, "I think we've got it," meaning he thought we had what we needed to have peace in the region. Phil also said that he would go to Central America the next day to visit all of the presidents. I thought that was a bad idea and I told Shultz so, but he disagreed and told the President that Phil should go. Weinberger, however, was against it and voiced this opinion the next day during a White House meeting involving Shultz, Carlucci, and President Reagan. In a sense, this matter was not his business, which must have infuriated Shultz to begin with, but Carlucci and Reagan agreed with Weinberger, and Shultz lost. Shultz then said, in a tone of voice that can well be imagined, that he would fire Phil since he obviously was of no use to the administration.

One more aspect of this episode gives an interesting insight into George Shultz. In presenting his case as to why Habib should be permitted to travel to Central America, Shultz completed his argument by saying, "But I have to tell you, Mr. President, that Elliott Abrams disagrees with this advice." There are not a lot of guys in Washington, in that administration or in any other, who would have done that.

This was a rare meeting in the Reagan administration. All too often issues were covered over and not raised to the President, and the President was not forced to make decisions giving clear policy guidance. This incident, however, is also an example of the kind of event that greatly embittered the Shultz-Weinberger relationship. (By the way, Phil didn't quit after that meeting.)

Going back to the question of how Reagan's administration functioned, I said earlier that Reagan was not his own prime minister, that he delegated a lot and was not, I thought, a very good administrator. Yet in many ways, the administration did work well, and I think one of the reasons for that was that Reagan did give what I would call ideological or political guidance, which conditioned many of the wars that took place within the administration at lower levels.

On personnel issues, that meant that I was able to hire Democrats because I could say, for example, that this individual was a Scoop Jackson type of Democrat, as I was at one time, and on the same ideological ground, even though the man or woman was a Democrat. It also meant that on an issue like Chile, you had to be careful how hard you pushed because you had the sense that the President wasn't fully with you. On Central America, however, you could push hard because you knew the President was with you. People understood that there were issues on which the President had strong views, and they knew how he would decide if certain issues reached him, even though he never heard about most of them. Thus, matters were generally decided the way the President would have done had he been an efficient administrator making 10,000 decisions a day.

NARRATOR: You really became the spokesman for the administration's human rights policy and were called on to debate Senator Christopher Dodd and others with a much longer presence in American politics. Laying aside the right or wrong of the policy, do you think the confrontational approach that you perhaps were forced to follow was the best way of defending that policy?

MR. ABRAMS: Yes, I do. First, the Democrats sought a confrontation on the human rights issue. They knew that the President's position was not popular among the populace and that they therefore would not lose anything publicly by opposing him on this issue.

Second, human rights was a caucus issue for the Democrats, and in both Houses the caucus consensus is to the left of the party nationally. This was particularly true during those years, and the position of the party on this issue was pushed left by people in the caucus into a deliberately confrontational status. Certainly, the fact that they sought confrontation does not mean that we had to give it to them, but in the end, I do not believe we lost anything by doing so. In fact, until the Iran-contra scandal, I think we gained from it because the Democrats were somewhat taken aback by the fierceness of our approach. In many cases they had never had an executive branch official actually tell them they did not know what they were talking about and that their views were blind and dangerous. Of course, after Iran-contra the political weight or balance switched from the President's side to the Democrats' side.

Also, Shultz—more than Haig, Vance, or certainly Baker—did not at all mind sending assistant secretaries out to face the opposition. I was out there more than Chester Crocker was, but he was also a good target for the Democrats on South Africa, and Shultz believed that we were the people who could probably handle the argument best. Certainly the President liked the confrontational policy. Had we tried a nonconfrontational policy, it might have worked better, but I would say that until Iran-contra, we were winning. Remember that when I arrived in August 1985, we won $27 million for the contras, and in 1986, we won $100 million. In

1988, after Iran-contra, we lost the vote for getting another $25 or $30 million by four votes, so I think had it not been for Iran-contra, the confrontational policy would have paid off.

I would add a further comment, however. How is it that the good Elliott Abrams became the bad Elliott Abrams? I don't think I underwent a change in personality; rather I believe there was a change of issues. The Democrats were not seeking confrontation on our human rights policy; they were seeking it on Central America.

NARRATOR: Negatives don't always prove anything. Does the manner in which the Bush administration handled Central America—though it faced different circumstances—prove anything one way or another about the wisdom of your policy?

MR. ABRAMS: I don't think so. First, until Iran-contra, we won a lot of votes on the Hill. If you think about it, the fact that a heavily Democratic Congress approved $100 million for a guerrilla war ten years after Vietnam is quite amazing.

Second, as you suggested, the situation that the Bush administration faced was quite different. By then, the Russians were pushing the Sandinistas into an election. The election strategy was one that we had also used on occasion. In Chile, for example, it was a great success. It is a terrific strategy wherever it is used because it is not just a strategy; it involves a real event. Thus the administration was smart to use that strategy. The question, however, is whether they were smart enough to know that the Sandinistas would not win, or did they luck out? I think most of them probably thought the Sandinistas would win. Finally, it is only 1990. Come back to me in 1992, and Nicaragua will be a holy mess.

NARRATOR: You have worked for three of the most striking political figures in American politics: Henry "Scoop" Jackson, Daniel Moynihan, and Ronald Reagan. Is there anything from your experience with the first two that, by contrast or similarity, bears on the success and the strength of Reagan?

MR. ABRAMS: I will make a strange analogy between Jackson and Reagan. Moynihan, on the other hand, was completely different in every way. He was much smarter than the other two, more educated and learned than the other two, and much more difficult to get along with.

Witnessing the relationships between Reagan and his closest advisers gave me an odd and almost eerie feeling. Scoop was beloved to all of us who worked for him, but his vices and limitations were understood as well as his virtues. For example, he knew a great deal about military issues, but he knew little about economic issues. None of us who worked for him believed that he had the kind of brilliant mind that Moynihan does. Thus, Jackson's staff had an interesting combination of love and respect for the man, as well as a slight sense of vulnerability on his behalf. For example, when he gave an interview, you were always a little worried they might ask him an economic question and that he might not know the answer or give a wrong answer. We always had a sense of edginess that people who did not love him as we did would try to trip him up. There was never disrespect, because we worked with him—in many cases for 10, 20, or 30 years—but many of us had almost a paternal feeling for him.

The situation in the Reagan administration reminded me a little of that experience, because many of the people closest to him loved him but also understood his limitations. They were constantly edgy about his making mistakes and about protecting him from mistakes. Mrs. Reagan is perhaps the foremost example of this.

There was also a difference between the two situations, however. Moving from the position of a senator to a president, you discover that not everybody around the president loves him. There will be many people around him who just want a meal ticket. Scoop's staff also began to develop some of this when Scoop ran for president. Then we had people who joined the staff because they thought he might win, or worse yet, didn't care if he won but thought it might be good for their careers to be on the campaign staff for a while. As the campaign turned out, it was not so great for anyone's career, but that is another matter.

While Reagan was president, there were necessarily a lot of people around who didn't know him at all and had no reason to feel emotionally attached to him. In other cases, people were just looking out for themselves: Not only did they not respect him, they disrespected him. I believe that by the time he quit, Haig, for example, did not respect the President, whereas Shultz always did, even when he thought the President was wrong. When the

President made a decision Shultz thought was wrong and others of us would say this is unbelievable and rail about it, Shultz would smile and tell us that we needed to get ourselves elected president so we could make those decisions. He would say that he was not elected president and could not make those decisions and would remind us of the special talents the President had that got him elected.

I'm struck by the number of people surrounding the President, such as Edwin Meese, who loved the President yet were pushed aside by people who had no regard for him but were more effective as bureaucrats. I don't know if there is any way around this problem, and I don't think there was a solution to it in the Reagan administration. An operation of that scale brought in people to whom the President's strengths were of less importance and to whom his weaknesses were more glaring. Although this did not happen much on Scoop's staff, I sometimes wonder if it would have happened if he had been elected president and we had to bring in people who had never met him before.

NARRATOR: We have kept you much longer than we normally do, but it has been to our benefit. We thank you very much.

III

THE REAGAN STRATEGY:
PERSONAL OR INSTITUTIONAL?

CHAPTER 7

ADMINISTRATION AND TECHNICAL ASSISTANCE: A.I.D.'S WESTERN HEMISPHERE PROGRAM*

DWIGHT INK

NARRATOR: One of the things that is always lacking in oral history efforts is a comparative perspective. A qualification that not many of our visitors are going to have is having worked in seven administrations (Mr. Nitze is another exception). Dwight Ink has had direct involvement in seven presidencies providing him with a perspective and viewpoint that makes for new insights on the Reagan presidency. Although, as he will tell you, he wasn't included on any continuing basis in the inner circle of the Reagan administration, he did touch that circle in three or four different ways. He was senior adviser to the Carter to Reagan transition, worked as the head of the Community Service Administration (CSA) and the General Services Administration (GSA), and was assistant administrator of the Agency for International Development. Finally, he looks at the presidency from the vantage point that is reflected in his succeeding Luther Gulick as the president of the Institute of Public Administration, the oldest and most distinguished group in the public administration field.

MR. INK: Thank you, Ken. It is my view that probably no one, including the President himself, has a full picture of any presidency. As I think back through the administrations I've been involved in,

---

Presented in a Forum at the Miller Center on 11 September 1989.

probably the closest to having a full picture of any presidency was Andy Goodpaster in the Eisenhower administration. He was very unusual. Therefore, the piecing together of people's viewpoints from different vantage points is probably the only way to begin to get a real understanding of any presidency. This is like the perspectives of the blind people looking at the elephant perhaps best illustrated with regard to the Nixon presidency. You hear on the tapes the ugliness, the lack of principle, and things that we absolutely abhor in a presidency. Yet, the President Nixon I knew held off influences, such as special interest groups, more often than any other president I observed. The courage he demonstrated in fighting those special interest groups is a world apart, maybe a galaxy apart, from what you hear of Nixon in those tapes.

I was not in the inner Reagan circle, so what you hear today is probably not quite as exciting as what you would hear talking with an Ed Meese or a Don Regan. I have been for many years on the periphery of the White House organizations. I've never made history. Maybe I have made footnotes on a lot of history. Therefore, you'll get a perspective from the periphery rather than the perspective of someone who had daily meetings with the President.

I did have the opportunity under Reagan before he was inaugurated to be a member of the Policy Committee of the President-elect Transition Team. I had responsibility for recommending the organization and management of the incoming administration. I was head of an independent agency, the Community Service Administration. I also headed the General Services Administration for a short time. Finally, I was assistant administrator of the Agency for International Development (AID) where I had responsibility for activities in the Western Hemisphere, including the implementation of the CBI and the Kissinger Commission. I was not responsible for the contras, I hasten to add. Every once in a while you luck out by not having a job. If I was ever lucky, I was lucky in that respect.

The Reagan transition in my judgment—and I've worked with all of them since the Eisenhower-Kennedy transition—was by far the best, although there was in some respects an overkill. I think there were more people involved in the agency transition teams than was necessary, and, as is almost inevitable in that kind of process, there was considerable unevenness in that part of the transition that dealt with departments and agencies. Some of the work was outstanding, and some of it rather poor.

The central part of the transition I found impressive. First of all, I thought the policy machinery that was organized by Meese and operated largely by Ed Harper—an official in the Nixon White House and later the deputy director of OMB (Office of Management and Budget)—was extremely effective. Whether one agrees or disagrees with the policies that came out, the machinery and the development of policies for a new administration were very effective.

I thought the extent to which future Cabinet heads were involved was very good, far better than in any previous transitions. I refer to it as a shadow cabinet, although it wasn't a shadow cabinet of the type you find in the United Kingdom. The meetings that Ed Meese drew together were significant and involved people like George Shultz. Although he was not the initial secretary of state, he laid much of the ground work in the international arena for the administration. The future OMB director and a number of other people, including Drew Lewis who became secretary of transportation, played very active roles as members of the Reagan transition team.

I was excited about my area of management, because we had an opportunity to lay out management proposals and principles before incoming Cabinet officials prior to the inauguration. We had an opportunity to lay out pros and cons with regard to certain reorganizations. These were questions such as whether there should be a Department of Education or a Department of Energy, how the Cabinet might be organized, and so on.

Of course, the major indicator of effectiveness is what survives the inauguration. It survived very well, for the most part. In the Ford-Carter transition, there was also quite a good transition planning period. However, when Ham Jordan and his campaign people rested from the campaign and came back, they shoved everyone aside. They took over, and a lot of very good work was either never picked up or picked up halfway through the Carter transition.

The most dramatic example of the Reagan transition planning surviving involves David Stockman's first budget that President Reagan presented. The Reagan administration was so far ahead of the Congress and moving so quickly that, although some of the techniques they used were not the sort anyone around this table would support or applaud, they were certainly effective in terms of achieving the objectives of the President.

The lowest survival rate, I would say, of the policy work in the transition, work which almost totally failed, was the work over which I was in charge. I don't know whether it was me or the policies I proposed, but the day before inauguration I was sitting on top of the world; about a week after inauguration the whole thing had passed me by.

After the inauguration, though, I did stay with the White House for a while and helped with some of the initial work of the new administration. Meese then asked me to head the Community Service Administration which they were planning to abolish. I said no. That was not a very attractive assignment, but I did write a memorandum on how I thought it should be closed down. My objection was not the fact they planned to close it down, but rather that I thought it should not be approached the way it was in the Nixon administration under Howard Phillips, an approach I thought was unprincipled and ineffective. So I wrote a memorandum which was shared with Baker and the President. Basically, I took the Howard Phillips approach and then recommend the exact opposite of what he attempted. The Reagan White House was so desperate for someone to do it that they agreed to what seemed on the surface to be counter to the perceived rightist agenda of a Reagan administration as it related to poverty programs, and the President sent my name to Congress.

One of the things that I included in that memorandum was the importance of relying on the career service, the people already in Community Service Administration itself, to dismantle the agency. This was something that the Heritage Foundation and other conservatives thought was the worst thing to do. These employees were largely Democrats, people who were opposed to the Reagan presidency to begin with. Further, they were expected to be demoralized by a presidential effort to eliminate their agency and eliminate their jobs, and therefore, it was alleged they would sabotage the President's plans. I felt, however, that this was the only way to go. The Reagan administration should not kill the poverty programs but shift operating responsibility from the national government to the states.

CSA was supposed to be a temporary agency to begin with. It was supposed to develop new methods of dealing with poverty and to raise the consciousness of the nation toward the plight of the poor. After it had been in effect for a certain number of years, those programs were to go back to other federal departments and to state and local governments. So my approach was not to defund the left, as Howard Phillips used to say, and it was not to eliminate help to the poor. Rather, I argued that the time had come to move the program back to state and local governments, closer to where poor people live and work. In order to do that, saving rather than killing the antipoverty activities, it seemed to me that the career people who knew the programs and had worked with the local communities needed to be asked to play a very important role. That was what we did, and it was an approach strongly supported by Meese and Harper.

At the first CSA staff meeting—by the way, I always had the career and political people meet together—I said if we got any pressure from either the Congress or the White House concerning the appointment of career people or the award of contracts or grants, I would regard it as a sign that this grant, contract, or individual was lacking in some way, and they were trying to make up for the deficiency through political pressure. Of course the idea behind this statement was to send a signal to both the White House and Congress that we were not going to deal in the business of favoritism. The signal got out. What I didn't know was that the Community Service Administration had been heavily politicized during the Carter administration and very possibly before. Every grant and contract had been personally approved by the head of the agency, often in an environment of secrecy. Political considerations weighed very heavily in those decisions, I was told.

We had one case in which an individual from California wanted to trade upon his association with Ed Meese when Meese was in California with Reagan, and I turned him down. My White House liaison alerted the White House to prevent this individual from appealing to Ed Meese. He never got anywhere with the White House either, and Meese thanked me for the advance alert.

Ed Meese, although of a very different political persuasion, reminds me a little bit of Hubert Humphrey in that it is very difficult for him to say no to people, although he can take a very firm stand on issues. Despite his strongly held political views, and

Humphrey also had very strongly held political views, Ed needed protection from associates taking advantage of him, just as Humphrey did.

During this early period in 1981, the first shock wave in terms of dealing with budgets and severe budget cuts was occurring. The word had often gone out from earlier presidents that there was no room for supplemental budget appropriations. Under Reagan, however, that message had teeth in it, so it was with some trepidation that I approached Dave Stockman to say that I needed a supplemental in order to close down the agency. Some of my political staff thought what I ought to do was quietly work around the White House and get the Congress to agree to a supplemental. We needed a supplemental because, if we were going to close down the agency, we had to have funds that were not there to provide for severance pay for the employees. There are a number of things that were required for a responsible closedown that weren't in the budget. However, I've never believed in going around the White House. You may agree or disagree with the president, but as either a presidential appointee or careerist, it is disloyalty to your boss and weakens the presidency. I wasn't about to do that.

To my utter surprise, after talking with Dave Stockman for about six or seven minutes, he agreed. So the administration did support a supplemental to help us close down the agency. By the way, I went to Stockman before the Congress had agreed to close down the agency. When I took the job, we had no idea whether it would be closed down. So I had to get Stockman's approval and lay the closure groundwork up on the Hill as a contingency course of action even before a decision had been made to close down the agency. However, the supplemental was not passed until the last minute.

All through that period of closedown we made an effort to emphasize people and employee concerns in the agency. Some money, for example, went to help employees situate themselves for new employment. We didn't have support from Don Devine, who headed the OPM (Office of Personnel Management), but we had excellent support from the White House. We worked very closely, not only with governors and mayors, as you would expect, but with Senator Kennedy and the Democratic leadership who had vigorously opposed the closing of the agency. As a matter of fact, I worked very closely with the national leadership of the community action agencies and very closely with those at all levels of government who politically were at the opposite end of the spectrum from the Reagan administration. My people thought I was going to get in trouble with the White House because of this strategy, but no one in the White House ever said they had any problem with it. That type of cooperation took the steam out of the political opposition and contributed heavily to the President's achieving his objective of closing the agency. I kept Ed Meese informed all along, so he knew what I was doing and supported it, as did OMB and the others. When I ran into real problems with OPM leadership, we had support from the White House.

One other thing might be of interest. My deputy, after he came on board but before he was confirmed, turned out to be an ideologue of the Howard Phillips type. I got quite worried, as several of my key political staff did, about what he would do when he was confirmed and had acquired some authority as the new deputy. I told the White House of my concern and worked out arrangements with the Hill, so he didn't get confirmed until about two hours after the agency closed. There was just a little squib in the *Washington Post* on the appointment. Of course, the *Post* didn't know the story behind it, but it noted with some curiosity that the deputy head of that independent agency had finally gotten Senate confirmation a couple of hours after the agency no longer existed.

I was unemployed for a short time after the agency closed down since I had terminated myself along with the others, but first I had an exit meeting with the President and with Bush. The meeting with Reagan was extremely friendly. He is very personable. It is almost impossible to dislike him. You may dislike his policies, but as an individual he is extremely charming. I must say, I did have difficulty dealing with the substantive issues in that meeting. He was very complimentary, but I wanted to talk about how the career people had carried out a very difficult, distasteful assignment in a highly responsible way. Later, I met with Mr. Bush, and he was very interested in this, an interest which is reflected in the support he has given the career service as President. I had a very substantive and satisfying meeting with Vice President Bush.

Placing the political people in other assignments after the closedown was a disappointment. Of my political appointees, the one who was placed most readily was the deputy I just mentioned. The two that I thought were most effective never found another job in the Reagan administration. However, a couple of people who were quite competent eventually received assignments.

After serving as vice president of the Synthetic Fuels Corporation from which I resigned in protest over its policies, I had a short stay as head of the General Service Administration. This assignment is an unfortunate reflection, by the way, on today's process of appointing of officials in Washington. I had been asked to come back into the administration to head the Western Hemisphere Foreign Assistance program in AID. The White House told me the confirmation process was taking many months, and asked me if I would head the General Service Administration while my papers were going through the confirmation process. I thought that was rather strange, but I agreed to do it. It took seven months for the papers to go through. You normally find this sort of delay problem regardless of whether or not the nominee is capable or noncontroversial. My Senate confirmation hearing was brief, and the vote was unanimous. It is a very difficult process, and it is getting worse.

Again, what I saw of the White House during the GSA assignment was very good, although most of my work on this occasion was with the National Security Council. I had no interference from the White House in terms of contracts. I was never given suggestions from the White House regarding the awarding of a contract or location of a federal building. I was never given suggestions of favoritism for agency employees. I couldn't say that for the Ford administration, because in the Ford administration I was pushed around quite a bit by the White House regarding space for certain agencies and personnel.

There was a major controversy emerging in GSA. Does "Tilted Arc" mean anything to you? Well, it didn't mean anything to me when I took the GSA job, but it means a lot to me now. The "Tilted Arc" was a part of the Arts in Construction Program that was initiated in the Nixon administration. This program directs a small percentage of money going to the construction of a federal building into art related to that building. Going back to the Greeks and Romans, public buildings were supposed to be buildings that the public could take pride in. You can't take pride in most of the recent federal buildings which are quite bland. Today, the budget won't permit architecture comparable to that of the ancients.

However, they felt a little art here and there might help add some dignity to buildings constructed for the citizens.

In this instance, one of the few open areas in Lower Manhattan was to be a plaza placed next to the new Javits federal building. There were to be fountains and a small statue on the other side of the building. What happened—and this occurred in the Carter administration—is that a sculptor came in with this iron wall called the "Tilted Arc." It had some curvature to it, was about nine feet high, and about two hundred feet long. It was made of rusted steel, and was located so that it bisected that little plaza. Well, you can imagine the feeling of the people who worked in the building and those living around the building. It virtually destroyed the plaza. Women going home after work in winter were really worried because of the dark shadow it cast. Of course, GSA had to clean up the graffiti. Nothing lends itself more effectively to graffiti than a rusted hunk of steel two hundred feet long. I also discovered it had been commissioned through political influence rather than through the normal review process.

There were many protests, and it just so happened that there had been a public hearing three or four days before I took over GSA. I had to make a decision whether or not to get rid of it. It turned out that the issue stimulated the art community around the world, and when it became known that I was seriously considering the unprecedented decision of ordering it out, I received a mass mailing from Germany. Their museums and art galleries said the removal would be similar to Hitler's book burning. I gave it a lot of thought, and decided that the rights of the artist were not as great as the rights of the public, or the employees who worked there, so I ordered it out. Of course all hell broke loose, but the interesting thing was that it was the only thing the Reagan administration ever did which all of the papers in New York City, from the *Village Voice* to the *Wall Street Journal*, supported. It was condemned widely by the art community outside of New York City, but in New York City, to my surprise, it turned out to be a very popular move. We kept the White House informed, but the White House never interfered. I think they thought it was better not to get involved. Whichever way the decision went, it was going to be unpopular, and I think they felt it was wise to stay out of it.

QUESTION: What happened to it?

MR. INK: It went into litigation. Among other things, I was sued personally for $30 million.

QUESTION: By whom?

MR. INK: By the sculptor, because he alleged I had ruined his livelihood. I think it did have a negative effect. Anyway, once it was finally settled GSA moved it out of the Plaza.

I came to AID after my stint at GSA. My experience here with the White House during my tenure at AID was very negative. What I have said so far has been extremely positive in terms of my experience with the Reagan administration, but I didn't have that same good fortune in my work in the Western Hemisphere assistance program. There was a lack of legislative initiative except when Ken Duberstein was in charge of Congressional Liaison. I should interject that I am talking only about my own experience. There was certainly legislative initiative at the beginning of the Reagan administration. Look at Stockman, for example. In my particular area of international relations there wasn't as much White House initiative as I thought there should be during most of the last three and a half years of the Reagan administration. Neither was there legislative initiative from within AID. If the agency had taken more initiative, perhaps the White House would have responded, but I don't know if they would have. However, from what I saw there was a combination of White House timidity on one hand and belligerency toward Congress on the other. There was also, if not secrecy, at least a reluctance to work with Congress and to level with the Congress in the way that I think is necessary.

I will illustrate the timidity concerning Congress by something that is very much in the press now, the narcotics problem. Just as "Tilted Arc" was a surprise item on my agenda at GSA, narcotics was very much a surprise item on my agenda in AID. I spent more time than I would ever want to spend in the jungles of Peru, Columbia, Brazil, Bolivia and Ecuador. I saw how the narcotics system worked, from the planting of the coca through the harvesting, through the initial processing at so-called labs, generally lean-tos in the jungle, and then to the planes taking off for the United States loaded with cocaine and crack. Interdiction and eradication were not in my area of concern, however; that was work for the DEA (Drug Enforcement Administration) and the Coast

Guard. Again, I think our agency was partly to blame for our ineffective legislation, but certainly the White House also was. It permitted Congress to take actions which, while understandable from an emotional standpoint, were in my judgment stupid, arrogant, and irresponsible.

Here was a problem in the Andes caused by the United States' demand for cocaine. In a very arrogant fashion we would tell the leadership in these countries to do things which politically we couldn't do in the United States. We told them if they didn't do these things, we were going to withhold our money that was promised to help them counter the cocaine mafia. It is one of the most arrogant and counterproductive things I have ever seen this country do, and I was ashamed to be associated with it. I fought this strange approach as much as possible, but not very effectively.

Of course, you don't see the decisive governmental decision making that you'd like to see in most of these countries. The culture tends to move much more slowly than we would like. There are all kinds of problems of that sort. The fact remains, however, that this was a problem imposed upon them by narcotics users in the United States, and people there were losing lives because of it.

Look at the justice system in Colombia. Being a judge in that system is the most hazardous occupation in the world, far more hazardous than being in the army. They don't last very long. I talked to a Supreme Court judge one afternoon, and he pulled out of his pocket a crumpled yellow piece of paper. It wasn't yellow from age; it just happened to be yellow. It was a death threat which began with his oldest child working down to the youngest, and then threatening his wife and himself. If he persisted in his efforts against drugs, if he had anything to do with the extradition of drug lords to the United States, for example, the threat would be carried out.

Their communication system is frightening. I had occasion to visit a research program in the southern part of Colombia which was funded largely by the United States. I was cautioned against going, but I insisted. The ambassador said we would not tell anyone we were going. The only one who knew in the embassy was the security man. The pilot didn't know our destination in advance. We arrived at the airport before the pilot was told where we were flying. I was to meet with a number of community leaders as well as researchers. When we arrived at our destination two hours later there was a message already waiting for me from the terrorists. It turned out not to be a terribly threatening message, but just their knowing I was coming despite the secrecy sent chills down my spine.

This is a bit of an aside, but it might be of interest to you. At the meeting with the leaders of this fairly large community in southern Colombia, they told stories about how members of their family and friends had been tortured, killed, and kidnapped. It was a chilling series of stories. However, after we had finished and had a little reception, one of them said to me, "I know these accounts sound bad, but there is something even worse from the standpoint of the future of this country. That is the number of young men and women who are going to the Soviet Union." This was before Gorbachev really took hold. He continued, "They are going to the Soviet Union, Eastern Europe, and Cuba to be trained. The Communist philosophy they are learning there is going to absolutely ruin this country." I thought that was interesting, but at first I dismissed it. Nevertheless, I called the group back together and related what he had just told me. To my amazement, all but one of them agreed. They said these kidnappings, torturings, and so forth are not as much a long-term threat to the country as what their people are learning in the Soviet bloc. On the spot I formulated a peace scholarship program for the Andes that was established and is still going today. I think the threat, at least temporarily, is not as great. Anyway, poverty and terrorism dominate the world many Latin Americans live in.

I have talked about having some bad experiences in the legislative area toward the end of the Reagan administration. Reagan, however, maintained a good deal of personal strength in Congress despite the contra affair. This was because of the fact that Congress and the Democrats feared his political strength, but also he did have a strong personal impact on people. As I say, he is a very likeable individual.

Nicaragua and El Salvador probably deserve a word here. I was very unhappy that we could not secure a place on the National Security Council agenda for anything relating to economic assistance in the Western Hemisphere. Poindexter was preoccupied with Nicaragua and contra issues. I recognized that these constituted a very important set of issues whether one agreed or disagreed with the administration. We were spending a lot of U.S. taxpayers' money in the Western Hemisphere, however, and the taxpayers deserved more results from their funds spent on economic assistance. I was trying desperately to shift the emphasis of this portion of U.S. assistance from a geopolitical basis to an economic basis, as was Peter McPherson, the AID administrator. In terms of our overall foreign affairs policy, I wanted to shift the emphasis to economic development, particularly to economic support funds.

I remember getting so discouraged that I told a National Academy panel in 1986 that the National Security Council, in my judgment, had deteriorated to the point where it was by far the least effective of any NSC I had seen during my years in Washington. I said there was one exception, but it was very temporary, and that was when Kennedy first came into office. At that time the National Security Council virtually went out of existence because Kennedy thought it was too formal and overly structured. Then after the Bay of Pigs and a few other things happened, Kennedy, being a fast learner, developed a very effective National Security Council, and it worked very well under McGeorge Bundy.

When I went into Elliott Abram's office on a few occasions, I saw this young colonel sitting outside. I never met him, but my staff knew him somewhat. He was Colonel North. They said he was a very effective individual, very action-oriented. They said that although he had a lot of strengths, he was one of those whose idea of gun control was aiming straight.

I had a major disagreement with NSC staff concerning how we use our money in El Salvador. Each year I had responsibility for about half a billion dollars going to El Salvador. Because President Duarte was a strong supporter of our foreign policy, there was understandably great caution and concern, both in the White House and Congress, about doing something that might upset him. In 1987, however, I held up all of our economic support funds for nine months, because I could not get agreement from El Salvador to use those funds in a way that would address their economic problems in a meaningful way. The Salvadorans said, "Well, tell us what we should do." I said, "This has to be your program. These are the issues we have agreed that you have to address: inflation, corruption, human rights, and so on, but how you do it has to be an El Salvador solution, not one made in the U.S.A."

After nine months I had a personal call from Frank Carlucci expressing his deep concern. Shultz was very concerned as well. I was called up twice by members of Congress because of their concern over the holding up of funds for El Salvador. I finally developed, with the assistance of their ambassador, a back-door personal communication with President Duarte, because the NSC–State Department filter was unintentionally distorting our position. With the help of both U.S. and El Salvador ambassadors, Duarte and I developed a strong friendship and mutual respect as we worked out a program with which he felt comfortable. He said he would implement the program, which he regarded as his own, and we released the funds. So it had a happy ending, but it was a cliffhanger for a few months. If you look at the program today, you will find that while El Salvador is not in the forefront of the greatest economic program in the world, it is implementing a very positive program, despite continuing civil strife.

Here is a case where, if we had earlier had an opportunity to get on the agenda of the National Security Council in order to make some conscious trade-offs and a thoughtful balance in the use of funds, I wouldn't have had to hold up these funds for nine months. I felt badly about the delay, because I admired Mr. Duarte greatly; he was extremely courageous. I thought he was trying hard to go down a middle road, attempting to minimize the actions of the death squads on the right while fighting the Marxist rebels on the left.

I felt keenly this lack of White House interest and involvement in nonmilitary matters. Although the needed balance in policy began to emerge after Carlucci and Colin Powell gained control, contra issues continued to be extremely time-consuming for these two able men. Had Poindexter put it on the agenda and had we lost, I would have been disappointed, but at least I would have felt the issues were addressed. To not have the issues addressed was something that I felt very badly about.

In summary, given the roles that I played during the Reagan years, I found the White House extremely good to work with when Baker, Meese and Ed Harper were there. I never encountered any political pressure when it came to appointing career people or when it came to grants or contracts. My experience in the latter part of the administration was not good insofar as the White House was concerned, until after Carlucci, Powell, and Duberstein took over, and things changed. Had I been in some other part of the administration, my experience might have been very positive.

NARRATOR: Do you think the transition was superior to others with regard to Cabinet involvement and other such activities?

MR. INK: It was superior in comparison with what had gone before. We will undoubtedly have even better ones in the future.

NARRATOR: Then with the implementation, things began to happen. You got a response you hadn't expected from David Stockman regarding the killing of the Community Services Administration. Some administrations we measure by positive programs. In creating a new program, you are encouraged when you get administrative response. With Meese, the White House relationship seemed to be good, but you were protecting Meese. If you had been trying to get Meese to initiate something, say this Western Hemisphere program, was there much to build on?

I was always astounded by what the Rockefeller Foundation did in Latin America. In 1943, first the three musketeers and then the seven staff people started the agriculture program. It was the cornerstone of the green revolution and programs that were to go on in so many other places.

We've been reading about Cali, Colombia and the Universidad del Valle. Cali had what many people from Asia and Africa felt was the best developmental university in the world. Two physicians gave up their practice and devoted their lives to starting this university. There were positive areas of development, but there you confronted the hard-line view. What kind of conclusion should we draw about the nature of this administration from what you weren't able to accomplish?

MR. INK: When you talk about the international area, it is important to recognize that in the earlier part of the Reagan administration, Peter McPherson was able to do some very positive things in the foreign assistance area with the support of the White House. I feel that Peter McPherson had the most effective foreign assistance program that we've ever had in the United States.

Later, things took a downward turn. When the Iran-contra affair began to preoccupy the White House, when we had people like Poindexter at NSC and Don Regan as chief of staff, there were some serious negatives that were not there in the earlier part of the

Reagan administration. At the very end, these people were gone and the situation improved.

In terms of implementation, it is important not to equate whether or not we like the policy with whether a policy formulation process was effective. The transition, I think, was extremely effective in setting the budget priorities of the new President. You may think they were terrible priorities, but the purpose of the transition is to position a president's administration so that it can move forward quickly and Reagan did.

The defense buildup was effective. One might say that should not have happened, but it was effective from the standpoint of presidential decision making. They closed down the Community Services Administration, shifting it to state and local government. It may be regarded as a bad policy decision, but it was a policy decision that grew out of the effective functioning of the transition. I would argue that this transition was pretty effective in most areas, even though in my particular area of management it was a failure.

It was a failure because the Reagan administration never picked up in the area of management once the inauguration took place. There were two exceptions. When Ed Harper was deputy director of OMB, there was a lot of emphasis on the inspector general program. This had some positive aspects to it. Unfortunately, there was no comparable interest in departmental management, and you cannot manage departments through the inspector general. That is a backup oversight system. The Reagan administration moved forward in some useful financial management areas such as cash management and the improvement of accounting systems. However, none of these administrative systems efforts made a bit of difference to the public. None of it has much impact on the effectiveness of delivery systems or the effectiveness of government operations. I think it was pretty much a failure because program management was ignored.

Actually, that area has been going downhill ever since Watergate. The management of our government has never recovered. By the way, it's not being picked up in the Bush administration either except in OPM.

NARRATOR: One of your predecessors talked about Cabinet councils. What is your assessment of these?

MR. INK: I favor Cabinet councils, but how they are used depends on the president. A Cabinet council would not have been of much use under President Kennedy. That was not his style of operation. Although Eisenhower didn't call them Cabinet councils, he did use them quite well. Nixon did not use them well. Nixon had the Domestic Council, which I helped establish. However, the way he and the White House staff operated, it was probably the best example of misuse of that kind of a mechanism. Despite this, I did recommend a council type of approach at the outset of the Reagan administration. What they did was set up a number of different councils. I thought that was too complicated. There wasn't enough flexibility. I was also afraid that it would concentrate too much power in the White House. I don't think it did.

One of the things I find disappointing in most administrations is the difficulty—particularly at the sub-Cabinet level—of getting people with public or private operational experience appointed as undersecretaries, deputy secretaries, agency heads or deputy agency heads. Some of these people turn out to be pretty able and competent. A lot of them are not. Despite all the rhetoric about management, it is not a factor that enters heavily into most appointments, and at times it is totally absent.

COMMENT: From what you've described in the field of foreign affairs, there were essentially two presidents under Reagan.

MR. INK: In my areas of responsibility, that was the case. I don't think that would be true overall.

QUESTION: Do you attribute this basically to Regan and his succession of Baker and Meese?

MR. INK: I think that played a role, but the National Security Council itself was more important to AID. President Reagan's hands-off policy was also important. Reagan, in Cabinet or NSC meetings that I attended, was neither impressive nor unimpressive. I never saw him nod off; he was always very much involved in the discussion. He asked good, although not generally penetrating, questions. On major issues he was a very important factor, and was a dominating factor on those matters he regarded as truly major issues. He didn't engage in minor issues, and I think that is to his credit. That will be a plus in any evaluation of his presidency. He should have been more heavily involved in intermediate issues than he was. The Iran-contra affair, when it began, was one of those intermediate issues that deserved more careful attention. Then it became an overwhelming, all-consuming issue, but it shouldn't have. From what I have observed of the Reagan presidency, I speculate that he didn't pay enough attention to some of the memorandums that came by his desk. With neither Don Regan nor Poindexter apparently helping him out in that respect, he was to some extent an innocent victim. Nevertheless, I think he should have given more personal attention to that intermediate level of decision making.

COMMENT: Don Regan told us that his office had no responsibility for foreign affairs or military affairs.

MR. INK: Which is very different from what he was saying before everything blew up. Very different.

QUESTION: What about his predecessors?

MR. INK: His predecessors were generally not involved in my area of international affairs. Meese was not much involved at all; Baker was somewhat involved, because as secretary of the treasury, there are important areas of foreign affairs with which you are involved.
    I have a very high regard for George Shultz.   I was disappointed that I couldn't get him to focus on some of these economic issues because he was confronted with so many crises. I had great difficulty even getting access to Shultz, but when I met with him, he responded. I felt very good about his judgment.

QUESTION: What's wrong with having ideologues, who understand the strength of the communist threat in the third world, in charge of economic policy?

MR. INK: I think you need a diversity of viewpoints in an administration. What I don't like is the ideologues of either the right or the left who are so consumed with their point of view that they will use virtually any means to attain their goals and squeeze out other views in arriving at decisions. This was the problem with the Iran-contra affair.

I am very much opposed to the rebels in El Salvador. I've talked to some of the rebels who were trained in Cuba and the Soviet Union specifically to disrupt the government of El Salvador. Some of them were taken to Vietnam to train. I talked to many of them who received money and help from the Sandinistas, and used Nicaragua as a staging area for action in El Salvador. The Sandinistas established a kind of underground railroad for much of the rebel leadership in El Salvador. Thus, I support very strongly the basic Reagan policy, but I think that in no way justifies the maneuverings, techniques, and secrecy that were involved in the Iran-contra affair.

In my judgment, you have to have covert activities, but those covert activities have to be in line with basic policy criteria. We forgot that in the Iran-contra affair.

QUESTION: I was interested in the comment you made about it taking seven months to clear some of these confirmations. The other day Elizabeth Dole reported that she was disappointed at this stage in the present administration. She has two deputies who have failed to be confirmed, which is hampering her department. My question is: What causes these logjams? Is it because of a divided government? Or is it that we have too many deputy assistant secretaries in the confirmation process who shouldn't be confirmed?

MR. INK: The problems that she is talking about involved people who should be subject to confirmation, in my judgment. There is a somewhat larger number of political appointees than there should be in the federal government, but Cabinet members should have a number of people that are politically appointed. They need people who are loyal and support the philosophy and the political agenda of the president.

The problems are several. First, in some ways this administration was overly confident, because it was really part of the last administration. I think they underestimated the problems of a new presidency, and I think confirmation of political appointees is the area where that shows up most.

I don't agree with some of the other things on which Bush has been criticized for not moving fast enough. In a number of instances President Bush has taken the time not just to think through the policies, but to lay important groundwork with Congress and with other countries. So, for the most part, I reject that criticism.

Secondly, Congress is not a fast moving institution, to put it mildly. However, one has to take into account that the Congress has been burned on some earlier nominees. In such a situation, you are going to want more thoroughness in terms of the reviews, and this adds time to the process. The democratization of the Congress also makes it more difficult for committee chairmen to crack their whips and move things through committee than in the past.

Thirdly, there is an interesting trend in this country. While in many ways our country and our people have become more permissive in their views on norms of morality in society generally, we have moved in the other direction with regard to our expectations and requirements for personal behavior of our public servants. One question that always comes up is: What would the press do today with respect to the personal life of President Kennedy? There is a substantial shift toward greater conservatism in what we require and expect on the part of our leaders, and this complicates the White House task of enticing people to serve in government and contributes to the time required for investigation and confirmation of presidential appointees.

NARRATOR: What do you think has brought that about? Is it the code of ethics? Is it the Ethics in Government Act? Is it partisan, political warfare? What has brought that on?

MR. INK: No, I think it is deeper, more complex than that. I think the Ethics in Government Act is a result of this trend, not a contributing cause.

In the financial disclosure area, I am on the fence. I have spent a lot of time filling out forms. At one time I was filling out forms still going back to my work at the Community Service Administration. I was also filling out forms for my temporary job as head of GSA, and filling out still more forms for what was to be my later job at AID. If I had been a multimillionaire, I never would have made it. I can tell you that. Fortunately, I am not a wealthy person, but it was terribly time-consuming, and I made mistakes. I was very busy, and the pressure in these jobs is tremendous. The hours are tremendous and you just don't give the kind of attention you should to filling out these pesky forms. My wife and I sent in forms that in two instances didn't match with respect to dates of purchase and sale. There is no excuse for that carelessness, but it happens.

NARRATOR: Why has it shifted to that from what used to be the main issue of clearance, namely, Communist affiliations? Why have money and sex suddenly become the primary issues?

MR. INK: For one thing, I think the public matured and recognized the Communist witch hunts for what they were.

I mentioned Hubert Humphrey a while ago. Humphrey got much of his political start in fighting the Communists. Humphrey knew a lot more about the danger of communism than McCarthy did, but you wouldn't know that from the publicity at the time. McCarthy was an ideologue who seized upon an issue that had some legitimacy and turned it into a serious threat to innocent people. Humphrey was first offered the senate nomination for Minnesota by the communist-controlled Democratic Farmer Labor party and refused. He wanted to be senator in the worst way, but he didn't want to get into the national scene on the coattails of the Communists. He fought the Communists, drove them out of the party, and got nominated in his own right with a party that had shed its Communist influence. It is the only instance in the country, by the way, where the Communist party had that impact. My point is that Humphrey knew ten times more about the real danger of communism than McCarthy did.

I think the American people began to learn that, and as they matured, they developed a much better perspective on the fact that the Communist threat in this country was more limited than many had thought. When you ask why our views on sex have changed in one way for the general population and another for our public leadership, I have nothing to offer. That's not my bag.

NARRATOR: When we started the Commission on Presidential Transitions, we thought it was the FBI clearances that were causing the delay, but the more we got into it, the more this seemed to be only one factor among many.

MR. INK: Yes, it's one factor. The FBI really was not geared up to handle all the cases that came at the beginning of this administration, but in fairness to the FBI they were being asked to do more. They were asked more questions. They were asked to go back and recheck to an extent they never had before.

NARRATOR: One of the things our commission talked about was giving people who had been in government a lesser clearance check the second time around. After having been cleared previously, why would you be required to have a full FBI clearance?

MR. INK: That's a brilliant question that I asked many times and never got an answer. It seemed to me that they should have picked up where my last clearance left off and simply updated it.

COMMENT: They do have computers.

MR. INK: Yes, and what I couldn't understand was why they weren't able to exchange information while I was dealing with three different sets of investigations, each moving forward independently to a large extent.

QUESTION: How do you handle the change in administration philosophy on foreign aid? For example, under Public Law 480 Concessional Sales, we had very specific provisions for family planning, population control, etc. Purchase orders were issued on the basis of their performance. Suddenly we've got a complete reversal. How does that now enter into our program?

MR. INK: Family planning is one of the issues which, as the Reagan administration moved on, became a stronger issue. You had a much stronger role played by the right-to-life groups. There was a shift in policy in which the role of family planning became far more sensitive and was redefined. However, it was still supported by AID in a more restricted way. So you did have groups, organizations, and people who had been somewhat caught in that shift of emphasis. Peter McPherson tried very hard to fend off the extremes of both pro-choice and right-to-life groups, and consequently was lambasted by both.

NARRATOR: We thank you very much, Dwight.

CHAPTER 8

REAGAN AS FOREIGN POLICY STRATEGIST*

PAUL H. NITZE

NARRATOR: Mr. Nitze, would you give us your impressions of President Reagan when you first met him and your view of him as time went on?

MR. NITZE: When I first met Reagan, I thought he was just a born loser, and I didn't think much of his choice of people. So I started off with a negative impression of Reagan, but over time I began to have increasing admiration for him. He had strong beliefs. You have to have real beliefs in order to be an effective president. He wasn't a pushover in any way concerning those things he really believed in.

This came to the fore at the end of his negotiations with Gorbachev. I think he won hands down over Gorbachev at the Moscow Summit with respect to that part of the debate which dealt with the general superiority or lack of superiority of a communist regime over a free regime. That was the important debate; it didn't bear so much on the outcome of the summit, but it bore upon world opinion.

I thought the best speech that Mr. Reagan gave at that time was at the Guild Hall in London after the summit. I was told that it was written by Tony Dolan. I thought it was a very good speech.

---

*A discussion at the Miller Center on 23 October 1989.

It got a lot of worldwide publicity. I had a feeling that Gorbachev didn't really recover from that. He continued to support the Leninist approach to the conduct of foreign policy. That was a crucial period.

QUESTION: What light can you cast on Reagan's behavior at Reykjavík? It seemed to me quite astonishing.

MR. NITZE: From where I sat it wasn't astonishing at all. When the Russians said that they'd like to have a meeting at Reykjavík, it was not very far in the future. The first question was: Should we agree or should we not agree? We'd also gotten word from remarks that Soviet Ambassador Dobrynin had made in India which were transmitted to us by people in the Indian government. He said that this was going to be a very surprising meeting, that Gorbachev was going to come to Reykjavík with very dramatic concessions. Gorbachev, he said, was going to try to go very far in this meeting, and then try to arrange it so that we would be the ones resisting his dramatic proposals. This would give the Soviets an opportunity to clobber us propaganda-wise.

Frankly, I took these reports from the Indians seriously. Supposing they were true, the question remained, "Should we go to this meeting or should we not?" It was my view that we should because we were hung up in the negotiations on many important issues. At that time there wasn't any real prospect of making much progress. I thought if he is going to make all these concessions, let's buy all his concessions but not get sucked into agreements that we don't want to make. Why not go and see what we can get out of it? You get as much as you can and if you can't get more, you don't get more, but you don't act improvidently.

Mr. Shultz agreed. So on the first day, Mr. Gorbachev did make a lot of surprising concessions which broke a lot of ground that hadn't been broken before. As I remember it, this happened during the first afternoon. They then decided to turn over all the arms control and national security issues to a subgroup to work on during the night. I was asked to head our group, and Roz Ridgway, assistant secretary of state for European (including Soviet) affairs, was asked to head the U.S. group on non-arms control issues. Marshal Akhromeyev was chosen to head the Soviet delegation on arms control and national security.

We were told all this at 6 p.m. and were told to meet with the Soviet side at 8 p.m., so we weren't given a lot of preparation time or guidance. We met at 8 p.m. with Akhromeyev and a team of four others. They included Velikov, who is an important scientist, and Falin, who has been head of their machinations in Germany for a long time. He is a very bright and able fellow and very anti-American. There were also Karpov and Arbatov. Arbatov was no use to the negotiations at all. We argued about all the issues until midnight and then went around again. We were getting nowhere. There was no agreement at all.

The crucial problem in the arms control field centered on Soviet insistence that reduction should proceed by equal percentages, item by item. My worry with this was that if you got reductions in the items where they were ahead, such as heavy missiles, they would continue to be ahead even though both sides reduced proportionately. What we wanted was an equal outcome on the two sides. In order to get there from where we were, with disparities in the capabilities of the two sides, there would need to be differentially larger reductions by the Soviets (or by us) in those respective areas in which we each were ahead. Therefore, the object should be unequal reductions in the direction of achieving equal and stable endpoints. It seemed to me that this was crucial. By 2 a.m., we still hadn't made any progress at all because Akhromeyev wasn't authorized to agree to this proposal. Then he got up from the table and said he was leaving. I was shocked because he didn't say why he was leaving, but as he rose from the table and walked toward the door, he said, "I'll be back at three."

White House representative Bob Lenhart and I decided we'd go to the hotel where Mr. Shultz was sleeping, rout him out of bed, and tell him where we were in the negotiations. We sat around for that hour talking to Mr. Shultz about what we should do next. There had been a disagreement within the U.S. delegation. I wanted to make a move toward the Soviet position because I didn't want to have it said that we just stuck to past positions. I thought we ought to make some move toward the other side, from a public relations standpoint if nothing else, but my six advisers had vetoed the idea. Shultz gave me only one instruction. He said, "You go ahead and run this the way you want to and don't pay too much attention to what the fellows on the other side of the delegation

want." With Lenhart from the White House there, I felt this was
enough guidance.

When we arrived back at the negotiating room, I was thinking
that maybe we could make some progress and maybe not. Then
Akhromeyev came back and it was soon clear that he had talked to
Gorbachev, and Gorbachev had given him permission to agree to
the principle of unequal reductions in pursuit of final equal
outcomes. That was a big breakthrough. I thought it was going to
be possible to do all kinds of wonderful things as a result of that
breakthrough in basic principle. We made some progress. We got
a counting rule governing the counting of heavy bombers among
other things. Akhromeyev wouldn't cover more than just a limited
amount of ground. We kept arguing and arguing until 6:30 in the
morning. At that time we had to wrap this thing up before the big
boys met because we had to brief them beforehand, get to the
ministers involved, and brief the President. The President was
going to meet with Gorbachev at 8:30 a.m.

So we got all that done, but we were still far from an
agreement. Then they met with Gorbachev and the President.
They made some progress that morning but not much beyond what
we had made during the nighttime session. It was decided to extend
the meeting by another half day, through the afternoon. It was also
decided that at lunch there would be a meeting between Shevardnadze and Shultz, and each could have three or four advisers. Over
the course of the meetings Shultz wanted to go through all the
various remaining issues and disagreements to see if he and
Shevardnadze could make some further progress, but Shevardnadze
wouldn't sit still for it. He said, "There's no point in that kind of
discussion. There is one and only one crucial issue, and that is SDI.
Will you or will you not agree to a ten-year period banning
deployment of SDI types of weapons?"

Before the meeting we had considered the possibility that the
Soviets would raise this issue. There are all kinds of ways to skin
that cat, and I had worked over those with Lenhart and some of the
others. Richard Perle sat down and wrote a note which he then got
Lenhart and Admiral Poindexter to agree to. They were on the
right side of Shultz, Shultz was in the middle, and I was to his left.
The note was handed to Shultz from the right-hand side of the
table, so I didn't really have a chance to look at it before Shultz
read it. After he read it, he turned to Shevardnadze and said,

"There is a possibility of our working out such a ten-year period, but I haven't had a chance to clear it with the President. I don't know whether he will agree to it or not." Shevardnadze wanted to know how he intended to work it out, so he explained it to him. Shevardnadze said, "Well, that's worth discussing. Why don't we take it up with our bosses?" This was then translated into language that the President might use.

The President went off with Shultz to this meeting but when they came back after an hour or two, they said that Gorbachev wouldn't buy it. So we fiddled around with the language and created something that might be more acceptable to Gorbachev but which did not really change the essential scheme we had in mind. The President used this version during the subsequent discussion.

I think it is true that the President lost track of what the essence of the U.S. proposition was and confused it with the idea of the total elimination of strategic weapons. What we were proposing was instead the total elimination of ballistic missiles. The total elimination of all ballistic missiles would have left both sides with cruise missiles and airborne missiles of various kinds. We thought that in that field we were superior to the Russians. The things they had which posed a threat to us were the big and small ballistic missiles. If you could get rid of all those ballistic missiles, then you would basically solve the problem of the ABM systems. You didn't need ballistic missile defense if you had gotten rid of all the ballistic missiles.

So we could agree to 50 percent reductions in strategic systems in the first five-year period and then the elimination of the remaining ballistic missiles in the second five-year period, but at one point the President said something about always being for the total elimination of nuclear weapons. Shultz corrected him right away and said, "No, that's not what we are talking about. We are proposing the elimination of all ballistic missiles, just the ballistic missiles, not all strategic weapons."

That was a minor flap, but I think that's what caused Gorbachev to say that the President had agreed to the proposition of the elimination of all nuclear weapons. He hadn't really done this, as Shultz had immediately pointed out. A great deal of confusion amongst the Europeans and others was caused by Gorbachev reporting that the President had agreed to the total

elimination of nuclear weapons within the ten-year period. So there
was some degree of confusion, but it was quickly straightened out.

Overall I thought the upshot of the Reykjavík meeting was that
we made more progress in those two days than we had in years. I
thought it was a very positive meeting. This was contrary to the
views of the Europeans and many others who thought it was a
disaster. I didn't think it was a disaster at all. I thought it was a
breakthrough of great importance.

NARRATOR: What about the last exchange between President
Reagan and Gorbachev that the media played up so much?

MR. NITZE: That had to do with the definitional problem
concerning what was a "laboratory." The President just stood fast
on it, and I think he was right. That was only one of several
problems which were outstanding at that point, so it wasn't that this
caused the meeting to fail. It was what the meeting appeared to fail
over. All that was played up to a level above where it should have
been. The meeting collapsed on that and other grounds as well.

NARRATOR: The other thing the media played up was Kissinger's
criticism of the lack of preparation.

MR. NITZE: It was true that ten days or less was all we had, but
I thought those ten days were well used. There also wasn't anything
that happened which wasn't pretty well foreseen. I thought the
decision to have the meeting, not to reject the opportunity, was
correct. I thought it was correct to try to get as much out of the
Russians as possible without getting sucked into a deal beyond what
we would be happy with. So I thought it was right to have the
discussion, to carry it as far as one usefully could, and to stop when
it was no longer going to be useful. So I saw nothing wrong with it.

It is true that Shultz had hoped that it would go further. He
was very much disappointed and showed it on that final TV
program. He had hoped we could do better than we did.

NARRATOR: One of the things that enters into any negotiation
discussion is the issue of experience. Here most of what we know
is what we've read in the paper. We are told that the Prince of
Darkness, Richard Perle, was unremittingly against any kind of arms

control. That's a picture that most of us have been fed. He says that you are his mentor and that everything he has learned about arms control he has learned from you. Here was a man with great experience and yet somebody who was associated in the public mind with Defense Secretary Caspar Weinberger's point of view.

The other thing that the media have kept talking about with regard to the players is that Shultz was prepared to go as far as he was partly because he didn't think that these weapons could ever be used. He thought they were enormously expensive and a drain on the economy. In most discussions he talked down nuclear weapons and was prepared largely for that reason to go as far as he was prepared to go.

QUESTION: What about the dramatis personae in the whole picture? Is there anything that we haven't read in the papers that would help us better understand all of this?

MR. NITZE: Acheson, Wohlstetter, and I created a little committee called the Committee for a Prudent Defense Policy which was devoted to supporting the executive branch in getting authorizing legislation for an ABM program. Nixon maintained, and I thought correctly, that it would be impossible to negotiate an ABM deal unless we had a program of our own. If we didn't have one, what was the point of the Soviets negotiating?

We registered as lobbyists because Dean Acheson pointed out that we were trying to affect the vote in the Congress. We decided not to seek or accept any money from anybody who was in the defense business because that would give the impression that we were prejudiced because we were being supported by people in the defense industry.

The upshot was that it was almost impossible to raise any money. All told, the amount of money we raised was $15,000, of which I put up half. What could you do with $15,000? I managed to borrow an office on Connecticut Avenue in a building just being constructed. The owner let us occupy unrented space. We got help here and elsewhere, but the cash expenditures we could make were limited to $15,000. We then got three graduate students who were either working for Albert Wohlstetter at the University of Chicago or were friends of his children or something or other. That's how we got Richard Perle. They then recruited a fourth.

Richard was a very bright student. We had four extremely bright fellows working, and they produced brilliant papers, much better papers than those produced by all these prestigious scientists and Nobel Prize winners; the four managed to run rings around them. This was just sheer pleasure.

The result was that we finally won by one vote. The ABM program was authorized by one vote. After that I asked Richard to help on the negotiation with the Soviets. I asked Richard to come and work with me, and he did for a short period of time, but then he met Scoop Jackson, and Scoop asked him to join his staff. He promptly accepted that invitation. For many years he wouldn't acknowledge the fact that I had ever hired him or that he had ever worked for me. He would not admit any relationship with me; I was poison to him. It was poison to him to admit that he had had anything to do with me.

He thoroughly enjoyed working with Scoop because Scoop was a brilliant critic of policies conducted by the executive branch, and Richard Perle is a much better critic of bad programs than a supporter of constructive programs that are hard to defend. It was his ideal cup of tea to work with Scoop and have his support in criticizing everything the executive branch was doing. He was happy as a clam in that role.

It turned out that he never was able to give up the pleasures of being a brilliant critic and take a constructive role. It was just temperamentally contrary to his instinct. He continuously hurt himself, I thought, by exercising his wit at the expense of people whose help he should have been seeking to get things done. It is my recollection that he never did get anything done in the sense of being for a program, supporting it, and overcoming the congressional opposition or other kinds of opposition and making it work. He never translated his ideas into a program. He really has never done anything other than be charmed by his own ability to outwit and be funny at the expense of others. That's his chosen art. I've never felt that because Richard was against me or that there was any hard ill will in it. He was just following his usual tendency to criticize, and he was much more effective than anybody else in criticism. I never held it against him as much as I did against other people who I thought really meant it. I don't think he held it against me as much as he would have if he had really disagreed with me.

At the end of Strobe Talbott's book *Master of the Game,* in order to make it a balanced evaluation of me, he put in all these dreadful things. He said I had cheated, lied, helped to deceive the President, and so on. The book started out being too favorable, and it ended by being incorrectly negative. The one person who came to my defense was Richard Perle in his brilliant review of that book. Richard put it exactly right. He said that I had done it correctly. Nobody else would have thought of it; no other review of that book that I saw did me justice. Richard was the one who came to my support.

So my relationship with Richard is of that nature. I've been trying to carry the ball and find support while Richard has been having fun as a critic. I think he has had much more fun out of all this than I have. I haven't really differed with him that much because in essence I think Richard is a very smart fellow. He did see what was up and what was down, but it wasn't any fun to be for what was up. It was much more fun to be down on and making fun of those who were trying to carry out this or that difficult task. I don't know whether I ought to condemn him more than I do, but I don't, because it wasn't crucial. In the final days he came to my support.

QUESTION: Many people say that Reagan had a short list of things he cared deeply about and worked very hard to achieve. Can you help us understand how "Star Wars" came to be one of those things? It's not one of the commitments he brought with him to Washington. How did that come to be something that he was as personally committed to as he apparently was?

MR. NITZE: I think he came to a deep personal conviction that the destruction that could be caused by nuclear weapons was dreadful, and it was politically impossible to support a policy which depended upon nuclear destruction. We had to get away from that and move toward a policy which would merit public support for an extended period. He thought the politics of the issue led to support for the effective elimination of nuclear weapons one way or another. Obviously the best way to do this was through the total elimination of nuclear weapons, and he really meant to get rid of all nuclear weapons. He did want to.

Some of us felt that it was improvident to get rid of all nuclear weapons. If you did that then anybody with a small number of weapons—like the Libyans, the Pakistanis, or the Argentineans—would be able to threaten all kinds of things. In fact, they would be able to do all kinds of dreadful things without danger of retaliation. The world would be much better off with a higher number of nuclear weapons in responsible hands, enough not to be subject to small deviations and unforeseeable events.

That was too complicated for President Reagan, however. He wanted things that were more absolute in their effect. He wanted to eliminate all these things or find some way in which to totally negate their possible effect. He wanted to get rid of the possible effects of nuclear weapons one way or another, and if you couldn't negotiate them away, why not make them useless through an impenetrable defense? So you achieve absolute results either way; he wasn't satisfied with partial results. He wanted to achieve dramatic, absolute results. "Star Wars" was an alternative way of achieving an absolute solution.

I don't believe in absolute solutions. They have never impressed me, but I think what I have said correctly represents what was going through his mind.

QUESTION: Were these the conclusions he came to after he had been in office for some time?

MR. NITZE: Yes, they were. I think two different groups influenced him with the idea that it might be possible to have an essentially perfect defense. One was led by George Keyworth, Reagan's scientific adviser, and supported by Ed Teller and some of the people who worked at Livermore Laboratories under Teller, particularly a scientist by the name of Russell Wood, a brilliant physicist and experimental designer. Another influence was Dan Graham, who had been director of Air Force Intelligence at one time. Graham had done a superb job of tracking down a program the Russians had underway involving experiments designed to develop a ground-based particle beam. Our people estimated that it had cost them $10 billion to build this facility out in the center of Siberia. We used to follow it day by day as aerial photographs came in of what was going on at this place. The code name for this was "Peanuts," a strange code name.

Danny Graham said, "Our scientists believe the thing is nonsense; the Soviets are barking up the wrong tree. There is no earthly way to make this kind of a beam the way they are going about it and give it any lethal capabilities." He then took the five theses of the opponents who were claiming that such a device proved it was impossible, and demonstrated that all five were incorrect. He demonstrated that there were no physical principles that made it impossible for a particle beam to do what the Russians seemed to be trying to do. That was a brilliant job by Danny Graham. He did a lot of original work that hadn't been done by anybody else, and with not too many people helping him.

On the basis of that report he came to the conclusion that we could develop such a weapon in a relatively short period of time. It could not be done the way that the Russians had been trying to do it. It had to be done in a much more direct way through what are called kinetic energy weapons. He dubbed his program the "high frontier" and was one of those who persuaded the President that this could be done promptly, wouldn't be too costly, and should be undertaken right away.

As I say, there were a number of influences that bore upon the President. He finally decided that we should do it. So he approved this and it was incorporated into a speech. The language in that speech was never cleared with Weinberger, the Joint Chiefs of Staff, the State Department, or anybody else. It was just fresh out of the President's brain with a little advice from these people whom I've mentioned. It caught everybody else by surprise.

QUESTION: Do you think that the President's advocacy was more a function of his being convinced of the possibility than of the arguments that were offered later, that it may not be possible but that the cost to the Soviets of trying to counter it would be so prohibitive that it provides us a bargaining chip?

MR. NITZE: I don't think the latter was in his mind at all. That was in the mind of Bud McFarlane. He thought it might be a good thing for the President to pursue SDI for the reasons that you've outlined; it would be difficult for the Russians to know whether or not it was possible, and in the meantime you could use it as a bargaining chip. That wasn't in the President's mind, but it was in Bud McFarlane's mind.

QUESTION: Do you have any thoughts about the administration's transition period and the way it touches on foreign policy?

MR. NITZE: Yes, I don't think we have done it very well. A lot of effort has gone into trying to do better, but none of it has been very successful.   Each new administration, even if it's a new administration of the same party, is devoted to translating its marvelous victory into a policy which is different than the past policy.

This was particularly true with Nixon during the transition between his first tour of duty and his second. After winning the 1972 election, he and his advisers thought he had a marvelous opportunity to carry out without restriction all the glorious things that he had wanted but hadn't had the confidence or political support to do in his first term. So the people who were viewed most negatively in the Nixon team had their resignations accepted during the second Nixon administration. He promptly asked for the resignation of everybody, including those in the Pentagon and in high-level positions of the national security business. He asked them to send them in right away.

I received a letter from Fred Malek, Nixon's director of personnel, asking for the immediate submission of a letter of resignation. However, I had received previous instructions from Mel Laird, who was then secretary of defense, that I was never to accept instruction from anybody in the White House. I was to take it up with him and he would give me my instructions. So I took this letter and showed it to Mel Laird and asked, "Do you want me to give you this letter of resignation?" He said, "No, not until I tell you to. I've told you that before. Why do you bother me with it?" So I didn't send in a letter of resignation because Mel had told me not to, but everybody else did.

I was a Democrat, and there wasn't any reason why I should be loyal or why they should have any particular interest in me, but there were some very good Republicans in the Defense Department whom I thought the world of. Johnny Foster was running Defense Research and Engineering. He submitted his letter of resignation, and it was promptly accepted. There was another man by the name of Gardner Tucker who had been the director of research at IBM. I thought he was one of the best scientists in the world. He laid the foundation for the new programs that IBM later turned out with great success. Tucker signed this letter without thinking to consult Laird about it.

So the resignations of all these important and very talented people were accepted, but there was none from me to accept. I was the only person who survived transition. So we had an entirely new arms control team, just in the transition between the first Nixon administration and the second Nixon administration. So it isn't just a question of a switch of parties; it is a question of changing administrations.

NARRATOR: We know what kind of president Eisenhower was, thanks to Fred Greenstein and others. Andy Goodpaster has said of Eisenhower, "Yes, he did delegate. He followed the military model, but he never forgot to whom he delegated." Kennedy was another kind of president who talked to assistant secretaries over the head of secretaries. Yet there are two contradictory images of Reagan. One is that he was somebody who delegated authority, leading to the Iran-contra affair. Another is this fantastic image of him that we hear about in the popular media that, influenced by his wife and an astrologer, he changed the course of America's relations with the Soviet Union almost single-handedly. According to this view, he took a great initiative in the arms area and wanted to be remembered by history for this achievement. Which of those two images is correct, or what other image is more accurate?

MR. NITZE: My own personal view is one of lack of respect for General Eisenhower and a late-developed respect for Reagan. I don't know whether that had anything to do with Nancy. My lack of respect for Eisenhower is due to the fact that I think he was a hypocrite, lacked courage, and had bad judgment. That's my view, which is not the popular one. I know that to have respect for Reagan is not a popular view either. You asked me for my views; that's what they are.

REAGAN'S TRIUMPH:
PERSONAL OR INSTITUTIONAL?*

DON OBERDORFER

NARRATOR: Mr. Oberdorfer was born, grew up, and went to high school in Atlanta, Georgia. He is a graduate of Princeton University. His first position in journalism was with the *Charlotte Observer* in 1955. In the late 1960s he began working for the *Washington Post.* Mr. Oberdorfer's career has been highly productive and has earned him considerable renown.

His book, *The Turn: From the Cold War to a New Era,* is already considered one of the major works in the field of Soviet-American relations. It is especially important because, in contrast to many other books, it suggests that there were actors who played decisive roles other than Reagan and Gorbachev. He is also author of *Tet!,* considered by many to be the authoritative work on that aspect of the Vietnam War.

Beyond that, he is someone who has a wide readership, particularly among scholars searching for leads to problems in their own work. His high reputation is well deserved. We are delighted that he could talk about Soviet-American relations, especially regarding the Reagan administration.

MR. OBERDORFER: I would like to begin by taking you back eight years to the fall of 1983, which in historical terms is like the blink of an eye. At that time the United States and the Soviet

---

Presented in a Forum at the Miller Center on 2 December 1991.

Union were locked in an intense confrontation that alarmed some of our leading scholars. George Kennan, perhaps the most eminent scholar of Soviet-American relations, wrote that the only way to interpret the behavior of the two countries was that they were headed inexorably toward war.

In September 1983 the Soviet Union shot down an unarmed Korean airliner, flight KAL 007, which had ventured into its airspace. Later in the fall, the United States deployed medium-range missiles in Western Europe for the first time under a NATO agreement, and the Soviet Union reacted by walking out of the Geneva arms talks. Yuri Andropov, who was then the head of the Communist party and leader of the Soviet Union, issued a statement that anyone who thought there was any possibility of improved relations between the two countries while the Reagan administration was in power should be disabused of that notion. In early November of that year, the Soviet Union alerted its KGB intelligence stations around the world to gather on an urgent basis information concerning what the central headquarters in Moscow believed was an imminent United States nuclear attack on the Soviet Union.

It is hard for us now to cast our minds back just eight years to the period when the confrontation was that intense, and yet it was only a short time ago. My book basically describes how these two nations managed to engage each other and ease tensions, thus ending the Cold War.

The Cold War was based on mutual fear, and neither side's fear of the other was entirely misplaced. What the conflict really represented was not just a collision of historical forces, but a great misunderstanding between the two sides. I tried to tell the story of how we emerged from that period of intense confrontation and angst to reach the transformed world today. I covered these events for the *Washington Post*. My most important assignment since 1978 was to follow Soviet-American relations.

When I came back from Japan in 1975 after covering that country for three years, I joined the diplomatic beat. My senior colleague was Murrey Marder. I was doing the Middle East and Murrey was doing Soviet and East-West matters. In the middle of 1978 he took a leave of absence. I asked him whether I should stay with the Middle East or take over East-West and Soviet affairs. He said I should cover the Soviet Union. I asked why, and he said because that was "the only country that could kill us in the short run." Such a thought tends to concentrate the mind. They have 27,000 nuclear warheads in that country even today.

I won't recount the story of how the leaders of the two nations began to interrelate, which is the only way to accomplish a major change in relationships between hostile governments. The most interesting events followed the death of Yuri Andropov in early 1984 and the ascension to power of Konstantin Chernenko. He was an apparatchik assistant of Brezhnev and was so sick from emphysema that he couldn't even raise his arm high enough to salute at the parade when he was inaugurated. He only lasted a year. Then in March 1985 came Gorbachev, who was a new kind of leader.

In the fall of 1985 Gorbachev and Reagan had their first meeting at Geneva. One year later they met again in Reykjavík, Iceland, which was perhaps the most dramatic and spectacular Soviet-American meeting since Yalta in 1945 or the Kennedy-Khrushchev meeting of 1961. The two leaders, their foreign ministers Shultz and Shevardnadze, two interpreters, and two notetakers sat alone in a room much smaller than this around a dining room–sized table. They bargained about the entire stock of U.S. and Soviet ballistic missiles, which were, in effect, the foundations of their national power. At the end, they even talked about eliminating all nuclear weapons from their respective arsenals. It was an incredible leap into the future and seemed utterly impractical at the time. It seems a little less bizarre now, since President Bush and Mr. Gorbachev are talking about large cuts in U.S. and Soviet weapons for the first time since those days in October 1986.

Next came the Washington summit in 1987 when Gorbachev came to Washington, Reagan's trip to Moscow's Red Square in 1988, and Gorbachev's surprise trip to the United Nations in December 1988 just before President Reagan left office. At the United Nations, Gorbachev announced first that the Soviet Union had taken a new path and was looking at its relations with the rest of the world in a new way. Second, Gorbachev said the Soviets were going to unilaterally cut half a million men from their armed forces.

By the end of the Reagan administration in January 1989, it was clear that the two nations were on a new path that would have an impact on strategic relationships throughout the world. I decided to write this book in the summer and early fall of 1988 after Reagan visited Red Square. It struck me that this was a momentous event and that I would never again witness anything as important as what I had seen take place in the past three or four years between these two countries. I wanted to go beyond what I knew at the time in order to learn more and record what I could for history.

There are many metaphors for the job of journalist, but the one that I like best has to do with icebergs. What we do is report the tip of the iceberg, that which is visible today. Our duty as journalists is to get as far down below the waterline as we can by getting to people who will tell us the things we don't see.

We know perfectly well that we know only a small part of the story. We never admit as much in public because it wouldn't help our credibility among readers, but any good journalist knows perfectly well that this is true.

With my book on the Tet offensive and with *The Turn*, I learned a great deal by returning a year or two later to see the people who were involved, especially those who were no longer in office and thus freer to talk. This semidetached perspective adds a vital dimension that news chronicles lack.

Philip Graham, who was the publisher of the *Washington Post* at one time, was quoted as having said, "Journalism is the first rough draft of history," which is a nice way to think about it. What I call "contemporary history" is the second rough draft. That involves filling in the gaps between the facts you already know in order to have a better understanding and broader perspective.

I had intended originally to end my book at the close of the Reagan administration. It had a wonderful ending: Secretary Shultz and his wife were watching the inauguration of Bush on television because they had not been invited. They then boarded a plane and flew to California.

The events of 1989 were so spectacular, however, especially the demise of the Communist governments in Eastern Europe, that I just couldn't leave them out. So, I decided to cover such key events as the reunification of Germany and finally ended the book with the Washington summit of June 1990. Many people have asked me why I ended it then, and the real answer is because that is when I took my prearranged leave of absence and started to write the book.

By then the great turning point in Soviet-American relations had clearly taken place. Even so, I did not foresee, and don't know anybody who foresaw, the events of August 1991 and their earth-shaking consequences for Soviet affairs and relations between the major countries of the world. That is another story for someone else's book. My book concerns how these two big "ships" managed a complete turn in course.

Who and what are responsible for what happened? All of you know, and I'm sure some know far better than I, that there has been an age-old argument among historians about whether the main movers of historical events are underlying trends or individual people. Clearly, both play a part, and in this case the underlying trends were very important. Among them perhaps the most important was the development of a global economy, which is the driving force behind most of the advanced national economies today. Soviet leaders knew that unless they could change their system and become a part of the global market, they would be left far behind.

I remember a conversation I had in Moscow in early 1984, before Gorbachev came in, with a man named Fyodor Burlatsky, who had recently been in Washington. He had been a speech writer and aide to Khrushchev, and knew Gorbachev and Andropov as well. In the middle of our conversation he said to me, "Do you know the country that bothers us most, and it isn't you [meaning the United States]?" I said, "No, which one is it?" He said it was Japan. I asked why they were worried about Japan, and he said, "Because they are in the forefront of the third industrial revolution, and we are nowhere." He was referring to the high-technology computer age. Soviet leadership, with some help from outsiders such as former Secretary of State Shultz, began to understand that they were nowhere and that they had to change.

A second factor that people forget is the demographic change that had taken place in the Soviet Union. On the eve of World War II the population of the country was two-thirds rural, and less than 10 percent had even a high school education. It was a country consisting mainly of peasants, plus some urban workers and a small elite on top.

By the 1980s the country was two-thirds urbanized, about the same as Western Europe. The standards of education, while still lacking, had been almost revolutionarily improved. A very high percentage of the population had finished high school and many had university degrees. Even though the country was still ruled by a Byzantine system with a very small group of people at the top, many more people were becoming aware of what was going on in the outside world and within their own country, and there was a tremendous demand for change.

The third big factor was that the Soviet and American leaders understood at least implicitly that in the nuclear age it was simply too dangerous for two such heavily armed nations to be at loggerheads with one another. Something had to be done to defuse this danger or else sooner or later there would be a clash that would be the end of both countries.

Having outlined these key underlying factors, we turn to the aspect of how the individual people interacted. One almost has to start with Mikhail Gorbachev. For all of his shortcomings, failings, indecision, and lack of understanding of economics and other factors, I think he will be regarded as one of the great figures of the 20th century. I don't have much doubt about it. While he could not foresee the ultimate end of the process that he began in his country, it was a matter of tremendous historical importance.

Kennan once remarked in the late 1980s that he and other experts on Soviet affairs were mystified that a person from a provincial area in the northern Caucasus like Gorbachev could possess such political ability and a grasp of skills and ideas. It is still a very good question. Several correspondents who have recently been in Moscow are writing books about Gorbachev's life and the background of his policies, and we will probably learn more about this in the next year or two.

Eduard Shevardnadze was another remarkable person who was probably responsible for more of these foreign policy changes than we yet know. Shevardnadze had been the Communist party boss of Georgia. He had not a single day's experience in diplomacy or democracy when his friend Gorbachev picked him to be foreign minister in the summer of 1985. Yet he became a respected diplomat and a "small d" democrat. Some of the things that he said within the Soviet Union are absolutely amazing for someone who had been an orthodox Communist figure. There had never before been a Soviet foreign minister who had gained such a high degree of trust and confidence as Shevardnadze developed with George

Shultz, James Baker, and other world leaders. This was an amazing change, and he remains a major historical figure.

President Reagan is also a leading figure in all this. In the course of writing this book, I learned some things about Reagan I didn't know before that helped to explain some of what happened. In the first place, I learned that throughout his term Reagan was much more interested in engaging the Russians in a dialogue than I had thought as a reporter. In public, Reagan was condemning the Soviets in the harshest of terms, such as "evil empire," and was the most anti-Communist leader that we ever had. But that was all on the surface; that was the tip of the iceberg.

What we didn't know was a fact concealed "beneath the iceberg" in large part: at the same time he berated the Soviets, Reagan was very eager to engage them. Even when he was condemning them with his harshest rhetoric in early 1983, he was asking Shultz to do what he could to become engaged with the Soviets because Reagan wanted to go to Moscow. He always believed if he could just get a Soviet leader into a room for a private talk, he could convince him.

Secondly, Reagan had an absolute abhorrence of nuclear weapons. He often said this, but most of us didn't take it very seriously. The image of him as a cowboy riding out of the West, chopping his wood and that sort of thing made us discount his repeated statements that he wanted to rid the world of nuclear weapons. Our perceptions changed after Reykjavík, when Reagan put the whole pile of nuclear weapons on the bargaining table. The "Star Wars" program, or SDI, was another manifestation of Reagan's desire to stop nuclear weapons.

I think Reagan knew in general terms what he wanted to do with the Soviets, but he didn't know how to go about doing it. He tried writing some personal letters to Soviet leaders, but it didn't have much impact.

The person who helped Reagan accomplish what he did accomplish in relations with the Soviets was George Shultz, who is another remarkable person. Shultz is an academic economist who was appointed to high political office. He is a very persistent, dogged person. However, he did not have, in my opinion, the diplomatic brilliance of Henry Kissinger. He is not a world strategic thinker, but he had a clear conception of where he wanted to go with the Soviets.

His persistence was very important in an administration that was greatly divided over Soviet affairs, where various factions were pulling and hauling. Everything that the United States did in this area was controversial in Washington. Even though the President knew in general what he wanted to do, Shultz was extremely important in getting something done. There were many other actors in the story, as is always true of diplomatic situations—some of them by virtue of their position and others by accident, but these four men were the most important.

Where does it all end? What happens now, after the August coup, the demise of the Soviet Communist party, and the very likely breakup of the Soviet Union into several constituent parts? How does the world deal with this? How can we even think about a world in which the Soviet Union, which has been the leader of one of the two great blocs in the world since the middle of the 1940s, is no longer an international player, and even Russia is not much of an international player?

We are just beginning to try to grapple with and think through all these questions. As a reporter, I find myself surprised almost every day and uncertain about what might happen next. This is essentially the reason that I decided to devote a six-month leave of absence from the newspaper to try to put together the story of this great turning point. I felt everything had happened so fast that I could hardly grasp it myself. If I can't grasp it, certainly the people who are not following it that closely and just reading the daily headlines are going to have trouble figuring out what happened. Somebody else will have to write another book on the period from shortly before the August coup to the present.

NARRATOR: There is a mystery about Shultz and his background in diplomacy, isn't there? Henry Kissinger said that when he had to give speeches on such economic topics as the International Monetary Fund or the balance of payments, he would get somebody to brief him. They would pound the stuff into his head and he would give a credible speech, but he said, "I never felt it in my gut."

Kissinger once said that the one person in the United States that he knew who was qualified to be president was George Shultz. That was before Bush came in, and perhaps even before Reagan. But he then went on to say that George Shultz in diplomacy was like he was in economics. He said he could not remember a conversation where George Shultz had discussed any issue in diplomacy with him for more than a sentence or two. Concerning diplomacy, Kissinger said he simply felt that George Shultz "didn't feel it in his gut," just as he didn't feel economics in his gut. Yet, Shultz is the man who accomplished this diplomatic miracle. How do you account for it?

MR. OBERDORFER: As I said, I don't think Shultz was any great strategic thinker. In Kissingerian terms, he was not creating some intricate balance of power in the world, but he knew what his objective was—namely, a much healthier, more sensible relationship with reduced tension between the two superpowers.

Shultz knew that to attain this objective he had to develop a relationship of confidence and trust among his own people and with the Soviet negotiators. He was a tough bargainer. He's a tough guy in many respects and is no pushover for anybody.

He began to believe through personal contacts that these new Soviet leaders were serious about what they said they were trying to do, while much of Washington did not yet believe it. For example, in September 1987 Shevardnadze came to Washington and asked for a private meeting with Shultz. Shultz took him and his interpreter into the back office of the secretary of state, not his ceremonial office, but the one that they really use for their work. Shevardnadze told him, "We are getting out of Afghanistan, and we are probably going to be out by the time your administration is over. We need your help."

Shultz took this to heart. However, after the meeting they went to a conference room in the secretary's suite where the two delegations were discussing regional issues, and the Soviet position on Afghanistan was just the same as it has always been. It was total nonsense! Shultz was saying, "Why am I hearing this? What is going on here?" But he believed that Shevardnadze was serious and that the rest of this stuff was just for show; it was a smoke screen. He said nothing about it publicly, but he urged other U.S. government officials to take this seriously.

The CIA, other intelligence agencies, and most other people in the U.S. government who were familiar with Afghanistan didn't believe it. The Soviet Union had never retreated under fire—why should they do so now?

The point is that Shultz had a rather deep interaction with people who in their own way were revolutionary figures in the Soviet Union. He had enough confidence in what they were telling him not only to believe it but to try to act on it.

What is diplomacy all about, anyway? Some of the great diplomats in history have been strategic thinkers, while others have been front-line doers. I don't know whether James Baker will end up being regarded as a great diplomat or not, but his role is that of a negotiator. Shultz was a negotiator in a different kind of way.

Let me tell one other story about Shultz, because I find it so interesting. Most of what I know about Shultz's negotiations, by the way, I did not learn while I was covering the story. He wouldn't talk about sensitive matters with me or other reporters; he wouldn't breathe a word of what he was saying to Reagan or what Reagan was saying to him. He abhorred talking about any internal administration discussions. It was only after he had left office and agreed to help me with my book that he began to tell me what really happened.

I had 13 long interviews with Shultz, amounting to 24 hours of taped conversations. Someone asked me recently, "Who were your sources in the Soviet Union, Sovietologists?" To the contrary, I used to be glad if I could see the second assistant door opener of the central committee, much less a real professor. I was fortunate that Shevardnadze gave to me the only book interview that he gave during his first term as foreign minister. He also persuaded his subordinates to see me. My other sources included five deputy foreign ministers and three members of the Politburo; I spent four-and-a-half hours in the Kremlin with Marshal Akhromeyev, the chief military adviser to Gorbachev.

The story about Shultz is that in October he went to Moscow on one of his negotiating trips. It had been agreed the month before when Shevardnadze was in the United States that on this occasion Gorbachev would set the date for the next summit meeting to take place in Washington.

Gorbachev and Shultz had a rather contentious meeting, and Gorbachev refused to set the date at the end of the meeting. Besides being an economist and academic dean, Shultz had a great deal of experience in labor-management negotiations and was good at sizing up people on the other side of the table. He was very shrewd on this.

As they left this puzzling meeting, Shultz said to the small group who participated with him in the meeting, "There is something different about Gorbachev. I noticed it in the first moments of that meeting. Gorbachev has always reminded me of a line in a poem by Carl Sandburg." Shultz was referring to "Chicago," the famous Sandburg poem about an ignorant fighter who had never lost a battle. He said, "Gorbachev has always reminded me of this fighter who had never been hit. But only a few minutes after our discussions began I said to myself, 'This fighter has been hit, but I don't know who hit him.'"

Ten days later they found out that the day before this meeting with Shultz there had been a big meeting of the Communist party Central Committee. For the first time, Boris Yeltsin got up and attacked both Gorbachev and Ligachev, who was on the other side ideologically. Gorbachev thereafter became a little vulnerable in his own political speech.

I know that Shultz is not making this up because I have interviewed the people who were there with him. Still, it seems incredible that he could sit at this table, observe Gorbachev's manner, and say, "This fighter has been hit." Shultz had a keen feel for the way people act on the other side of the table.

Many of you probably knew Bryce Harlow, a key aide to Republican presidents. Shultz told the story of going to see Bryce Harlow soon after arriving in Washington as secretary of labor for Nixon's first administration. Harlow said to him, "Trust is the coin of the realm." If you are going to deal with people, you have to trust them. There were people whom Shultz came not to trust, but they weren't around too long in his State Department.

QUESTION: I wonder if we were just plain lucky to have had people like Shultz and Reagan running this country at a crucial time, and whether we could therefore in the reverse luck of the draw once again find ourselves on the brink of apocalypse as you described in 1983? Do we have some sort of mystique that enables us to muddle through with pygmies in charge instead of giants?

MR. OBERDORFER: I don't want to be misunderstood in my feelings for Reagan. I'm no fan of President Reagan in many respects. I think what he did with the economy was a disaster, and allowing the United States to go so deeply into debt was absolutely irresponsible. There were many other Reagan policies with which I disagreed.

In this particular field, however, in a funny way Reagan was the right man at the right time. Because he was the most right-wing president we had ever had, it was easier for him to make an accommodation with the Soviet Union than a centrist or liberal president. Otherwise, there would have been someone like Ronald Reagan on his right screaming that we were giving up everything to the Russians. On balance, I do think he did a fine job in the way things came out with the Soviet Union.

I think implied in your question is whether we might go back to confrontation with the Soviet Union. I think the answer is definitely no, it will never be the same. True, there could be great dangers for the rest of the world in the situation in the Soviet Union because of their nuclear weapons and other things. There will indeed be many unforeseeable consequences of the collapse of one of the great empires of our time. But the Soviet Union will not revert to leading a bloc of nations ideologically committed to confrontation with the West, at least in the foreseeable future. There no longer exists the comprehensive threat to peace that we perceived communism posed.

Regarding our current leadership, up until a month ago I would have said that in foreign policy Bush was about as good a president as we could get. He knows his stuff, is interested, and takes a clear position on foreign affairs. The administration, however, has suddenly plunged into some kind of crisis within itself as to what it is going to do.

I was absolutely stunned that the members of Congress who proposed an appropriation bill to assist the Soviet Union in dismantling their nuclear weapons could not get any expression of support from Bush. He just took a dive on the whole issue. I wrote about this recently in the *Washington Post* Outlook section. I don't know what Bush is likely to do now. I fear that we are going to have another year, or perhaps five years, of immobility because the administration is so stunned by the perception of economic reversals in the United States.

QUESTION: Would the failure of the Russian military to act to fill a vacuum be due merely to the failure of the economic and industrial system in Russia? Why haven't they done something?

MR. OBERDORFER: There was no consensus in the Russian military about what to do, and besides, there is not much of a history in that country of the military playing a decisive role in politics. Some military leaders backed the August coup; others did not. I think that if the economic circumstances continue to deteriorate and the people of the Soviet Union face ever-bleaker prospects as the state breaks up, there is a great danger that some other force, military or nonmilitary, will try to assert control and say to the people of the country, "We offer a way out." It is hard to imagine a collapse of authority taking place without somebody trying to provide some kind of leadership. The present Soviet military leaders, however, definitely disapprove of any attempted coup or other such use of its power for political ends. Whether that disinclination will continue to prevail in the future, I don't know.

QUESTION: You began by speaking of the crisis mood of 1983. Beginning in January 1984, the tone of Reagan's public statements and speeches changed completely. There was a very sudden shift in emphasis toward accommodation and summit meetings. I wonder if you have any knowledge as to what may lie behind that shift.

MR. OBERDORFER: I have a good deal of knowledge about it. I won't go into the details that are set forth in the book, but starting in the spring of 1983 some of the political advisers around Reagan looked forward to the 1984 election year and warned that a confrontational posture with the Soviets might cost votes. Moreover, Reagan had always thought that the United States should first build up the military and then negotiate from a position of strength, and there was a sense that he had done that. In the first two years the military buildup had proceeded, and it was now time to begin negotiations.

A person could make that claim in retrospect, but you would have to question whether they were saying the same thing at the time. To me, the most interesting and compelling evidence came from Jack Matlock, who at the time was the U.S. ambassador to one of the Eastern European countries and later became ambassador to the Soviet Union. He was called back to Washington and asked by Bill Clark and Bud McFarlane to take the job of head of Soviet and European affairs on the National Security Council staff. They told him that this was an important post because the military buildup had now gone far enough, so it was time to get down to negotiations.

Reagan actually tried to begin this in August 1983 when he wrote a letter to Andropov along these lines, but shortly thereafter the Soviets shot down Korean Airlines flight 007. That fall there was horrible tension over this incident, the missile situation, and everything else, and it wasn't until early 1984 that he was able to reverse the diplomatic trend. You are correct in saying that there was a definite shift in the wind, not only in Washington but in Moscow as well.

QUESTION: You have given us a wonderful overview of the long-term trends. You have also commented on the military buildup under the Reagan administration. Was our military buildup designed to spend the Soviets into the ground? Has this tremendous military buildup contributed to what is happening in the Soviet Union today?

MR. OBERDORFER: This has become a very controversial issue. Many Americans did not approve of the military buildup and thought it was a waste of money. There was particularly intense political argument over the SDI question.

My conclusion is that the military buildup, especially the SDI and high-technology parts of the buildup, was a contributing factor to the Soviet decision to take a new road. I don't think it was the central factor. I think the greater factors were things that I have already mentioned—the economic circumstances, the social and demographic changes within the Soviet Union, and the sense that the nuclear arms race was just too dangerous. The last thing they thought they could afford was a high-technology arms race with the United States.

What Gorbachev did at Geneva and especially at Reykjavík was to try at all costs to get Reagan to stop the SDI program. That was his central objective. I think the Soviets feared this new type of competition that would have cost them dearly and which they could not possibly have won. So I do think it was a factor. In the future, some person who has more erudition than I will have to figure out how much of a factor.

QUESTION: Now that Gorbachev's influence has diminished and there are new players in the field such as Yeltsin and other leaders of the various republics—for example, the Ukraine—what happens to the hot line between Washington and Moscow?

MR. OBERDORFER: At the moment it goes from the Pentagon to the headquarters of the Soviet military. I think we still need it. In fact, I think we need more hot lines to the Ukraine, Kazakhstan, and other republics.

You probably read in the paper that the *Bulletin of the Atomic Scientists* a few days ago moved their minute hand of the "doomsday clock" back as far as it has ever been because of what has happened. I might have been inclined to move it a little in the other direction because I think the idea of 27,000 nuclear warheads in a country that is coming apart is not one that is particularly comforting. It is hard to believe that this chaotic situation is not going to jeopardize central control over these horrible weapons.

I don't know how many of you have ever been to Hiroshima or Nagasaki, but I visited these cities while I was a correspondent in Japan. The museums there show the destruction caused by one nuclear weapon that is merely a toy compared to today's weapons. The thought of these weapons being out of control just terrifies me. We need to keep this hot line and have some other smaller branch hot lines.

QUESTION: Would you comment on the personal and working relationship between Shevardnadze and Gorbachev? How well do they work together?

MR. OBERDORFER: In the period I covered they worked very closely together. What I don't know is to what extent the initiative for various proposals came from Shevardnadze. We know, for example, that Shevardnadze was chairman of the Politburo Commission on Afghanistan. What we don't know is how that commission worked. We know it decided that the Soviet Union should get out of Afghanistan, but how did it reach that decision? Gorbachev may have developed the strategy for withdrawing from Afghanistan, or he may have said to his friend Shevardnadze, "We know where we want to go. You make it happen!" We don't know.

In December 1990 Shevardnadze came to feel that Gorbachev was not backing him up. Gorbachev had turned to the right that fall, and there were increasing attacks on Shevardnadze. Shevardnadze felt that Gorbachev was letting this happen and not standing up as he should, and Shevardnadze resigned in that dramatic speech where he said there was a possibility of dictatorship in the country.

He didn't tell Gorbachev what he was going to do ahead of time. He had tried to resign once before, but Gorbachev talked him out of it. From then on through most of this year he was an outside critic, a friendly critic in some respects, but speaking rather openly of Gorbachev's failings. About two weeks ago Gorbachev convinced him to come back.

QUESTION: Wasn't it a surprise that Gorbachev wanted him to come back?

MR. OBERDORFER: It was not a surprise to me that he wanted him. It was a surprise to me that Shevardnadze agreed.

COMMENT: He didn't have to work with Gorbachev. He could have continued in some other way.

MR. OBERDORFER: He was head of an institute, but I think he came to realize his institute didn't have much impact on things. It was at a time of revolutionary change in his country, and I imagine it was hard for him to sit on the sidelines. Gorbachev probably appealed to him by saying (this is a guess), "Look, Eduard, you know this is the moment when the country is either going to continue or everything is going to fall apart. I need you."

It is interesting that his first major act as foreign minister was to announce that he would visit the capitals of all 12 republics. He understands where the problem is and where the priorities are. They are not in Paris, London, or Washington, but rather in the Ukraine, Kazakhstan, Armenia, Azerbaijan, and the other republics. He is a good politician, so if anyone has a chance to try to work constructively with these national groups, it is Shevardnadze. Whether he will be able to succeed, I don't know; I doubt it.

QUESTION: Do you feel that Gorbachev will be out of office eventually?

MR. OBERDORFER: Whether it is by resignation or some other method such as ouster, I don't expect him to be around by this time next year.

QUESTION: Do you think there will be a replacement for him, a hard-line person?

MR. OBERDORFER: No one quite knows what the new system will be like or what kind of central authority there will be. Very shortly the Russian Republic is going to take over paying all the bills (to the extent they are paid at all) for the main central governmental agencies. That will give them control over those agencies. So, what will be left for a central coordinating authority to do? It is going to be a little like the Articles of Confederation period in early U.S. history. There will be the need for some coordinating mechanism. Who can do it? What are the ground rules going to be and under what circumstances? Gorbachev clearly has the greatest talent for this kind of thing, but will he be willing to remain in what is mostly a figurehead role over a long period of time? I doubt he would play second fiddle to Yeltsin, with whom he doesn't really get along.

COMMENT: It is almost an embarrassment to him.

MR. OBERDORFER: Yes, but to his credit, he is not thinking in terms of pride or embarrassment. He keeps seeing possibilities to salvage the situation that no one else seems to see. Maybe that is good.

QUESTION: On the nuclear side, did I hear you correctly when you spoke of events in 1983? I remember the crisis over the Korean airliner, and things were tense, but I don't think there was any notion in this country that Russia thought we were about to launch a nuclear attack. That is sort of a misconception.

MR. OBERDORFER: We didn't know it then. We know it now only because the KGB station chief in London, a man named Oleg

Gordievsky, was secretly working for Western intelligence. When he defected several years later, his story became public. The Soviets actually alerted some of their nuclear-capable aircraft in Eastern Europe to be ready to take off. It was frightening! The government knew it within a few weeks because of Gordievsky. Reagan alludes to it vaguely in his memoirs; other people were much more conscious of it, and the CIA did some evaluations on whether there was a serious danger. Reagan said to McFarlane, "You know, I can't believe that these people really think we are going to attack them. Why would they think that?"

But some people in Moscow evidently did. In the next year or two as the Soviet archives are opened and people become more willing to talk, we will probably learn more about why they thought this, and what really happened in that period. It is rather gripping that they thought they were about to be attacked.

QUESTION: If the Soviet Union is calling back Shevardnadze, who negotiated so well for them, why aren't we calling back our secretary of state who negotiated so well with him?

MR. OBERDORFER: We have a secretary of state who negotiated pretty well with Shevardnadze in the first two years of the Bush administration. Baker had and continues to have an excellent relationship with Shevardnadze.

COMMENT: But it was George Shultz who thought through the plan that still must be carried out successfully.

MR. OBERDORFER: That is true. I have a favorite phrase about journalism that applies in a certain way to the field of government. I have always been fond of quoting the dedication to a book written by A. J. Liebling, who was the great critic of the press for the *New Yorker* years ago. His dedication said, "For a school for publishers, without which no school for journalists can have any meaning."

In the end, it is the president who determines the foreign policy of the United States; Congress and the State Department play a subordinate role. The president must be comfortable with his secretary of state and other chief negotiators. He has to have the relationship with them that makes it possible for them to go out and work on his behalf.

In this particular case, George Bush and James Baker probably have the closest relationship that any president and secretary of state have had since the beginning of the republic. Jim Baker was Bush's campaign manager for the Senate race in Texas, for president in 1980 when he was beaten by Reagan, and in 1988. They are very close friends.

We also have a different arrangement for running foreign policy today. In most cases since World War II, the secretary of state has been an expert on foreign affairs, or becomes so if he isn't already when he takes office; the president is usually an expert on politics.

The secretary of state, secretary of defense, and national security adviser meet with the president and explain to him the main considerations of a given problem in an overseas area. Normally the president follows their recommendations.

In this case, the President is an expert on foreign policy. He has a good idea of what he wants to do. He knows all these places since he has traveled almost everywhere in the world. He probably knows half of the senior-level diplomats. The secretary of state happens to be an expert on American politics. Bush gives more specific direction to diplomacy than any president has since Nixon. The secretary of state thus serves as the chief negotiator. He's an adviser to a degree, but I think less so than has usually been the case.

Every president needs an organization and staffing that suits his own personality and circumstances. Just because George Shultz was successful under Ronald Reagan doesn't mean he would be that successful under Mr. Bush.

NARRATOR: Did Shultz ever explain why he thought he wasn't invited to the inauguration? That seems to go one step beyond simply not conferring with the former secretary of state during a transition to a new administration. Was there a Bush-Shultz relationship that figured into your study in any way?

MR. OBERDORFER: I asked him this and he said he did not know why he was not invited. Bush's relationship with Shultz for the most part was pretty good because the two men stood on the same side of most issues.

They did have a falling out, however, over the Iran-contra affair. Bush felt that Shultz was not being loyal enough to the President, and was protecting his own position. Shultz felt that Reagan and the administration were tremendously mistaken in trying to do what they were doing. He had been opposed to it from the beginning, and he said so rather outspokenly. But I don't believe that really accounts for it because people in politics always disagree about something. They are all grownups.

I think the Bush administration basically wanted to show it wasn't just a third Reagan administration. They wanted to get the old guys out of town as fast as possible. It may have just been an oversight, but I don't know. It was rather bizarre that a man who had served six-and-a-half years as secretary of state should be in effect shunted out of town. This was the longest that anyone had served as secretary of state in the postwar period except for Dean Rusk and John Foster Dulles.

QUESTION: Given the momentum of events in the latter part of 1988 and the presumed involvement of Bush's people who served under Reagan, why did it seem to take the new administration so long to get organized and march off in a new direction or to respond to the initiatives of the Soviet Union?

MR. OBERDORFER: Bush was very cautious and felt that the Reagan administration had gone too far to fast toward the end of its term. He was appalled by the rashness of the proposals at Reykjavík. He didn't like the political aura that developed between the United States and the Soviet Union. Let's not forget, he didn't have the same right-wing credentials that Reagan had and was vulnerable to attack from that direction. So, in the beginning of his term he was extremely cautious, and the administration was strangely slow in organizing itself. One would think it would be easy since they were taking over from another Republican administration, but it didn't work that way.

It was only in the summer of 1989, when Baker really began to engage with Shevardnadze and Gorbachev and things began to change in Eastern Europe, that the administration got itself together. I believe it took so long mainly because of two factors: first, Bush's caution, and second, the administration's slowness in appointing people to important positions.